NO BULL SELLING

NO
BULL
SELLING

Hank Trisler

Frederick Fell Publishers, Inc.
New York, New York

For information address:

Frederick Fell Publishers, Inc.
386 Park Avenue South
New York, New York 10016

Published simultaneously in Canada by Fitzhenry & Whiteside, Limited, Toronto

International Standard Book Number: 0-8119-0484-9
Library of Congress Catalog Card Number:

Manufactured in the United States of America
1 2 3 4 5 6 7 8 9 0

To Barbara.
Without her support,
encouragement,
and love,
this would still be a dream.

CONTENTS

A FOREWORD FROM OG MANDINO

I envy you. You—holding this book!

You're in for a shock . . . a pleasant, delicious, nice-feeling shock filled with surprises, smiles, and more, much more. Enough down-to-earth information and ammunition to make you as good a professional salesman or saleswoman as you want to be. And more? Yes! Because just being a super salesperson isn't worth any more than a discarded beer can unless all of you is fulfilled in the process.

Up front you should know that my views are biased. I happen to be a Hank Trisler "junkie." Ever since I first heard him speak several years ago at a National Speakers Association winter workshop for many of the top professional speakers in this country, I never miss an opportunity to listen to this wise and witty man even if I have to pick up the tab for drinks or dinner in order to get him motivated enough to share his ideas and pungent truths.

There are hundreds of sales books available to you at your favorite bookstore or library. If you're truly interested in furthering your selling career you have probably waded through several of them. Surprise! After four or five of these often very dull volumes you suddenly realize that not a one of them contains an original thought—they are all "refried" versions of countless sales books that appeared before and they're all singing the same tunes, off key as far as this turbulent era is concerned.

Not this book—and that's why I envy you the "Oh wow!" discovery you're about to make when you begin reading Trisler. Hank is that rare species, a constructive debunker. He demolishes some of the old and hallowed principles of salesmanship like positive attitudes, goal-setting with time limits, and canned pitches, and substitutes, for you, simple, powerful methods that he *knows* will work because he's been "out there" a long time and he's used them again and again.

Don't peek now, but Chapter 12, "Let Me Show You How It Works," has got to be a classic in the field of sales literature. When you begin to use the principles you will find in this hilarious and yet serious chapter your sales will probably begin to earn you the king-size checks you deserve whether you're selling Mercedes or Amway or tract homes in North Dakota.

And wait until you get to Chapter 15, "Keeping The Wheels On." In the past twenty years I have probably read or reviewed at least five hundred books on sales and none of them, as far as I can recall, ever took the time to give you the tender loving advice that Hank Trisler shares with you to cap off what has to be the finest and *most honest* book on salesmanship I have read in a long, long time.

If I were still in sales management I would rush out, right now, and buy a copy of this classic for everyone under my supervision. It would be the best damn investment I could make . . . in *my own* future.

OG MANDINO
Author, *The Greatest
Salesman in the World*

INTRODUCTION

"I am not saying that chance doesn't sometimes open the door. But luck belongs to the good players."

—*Bernard Baruch*

The canned pitch is dead—a thing of the dimly remembered past which haunts us even today. The main problem with the canned pitch is that you can learn your lines perfectly, but the customers keep forgetting theirs.

The canned pitch was all we had in the mid-twentieth century and was predicated on the assumption that salespeople had better know their product or service flat and be able to tell their story in a convincing manner. We thought it worked well, no doubt because it was all we had.

Today's buyer is better educated, more intelligent, and more sophisticated than any we have ever seen before. The old ways of selling fail with baffling regularity. Our customers need to be understood, not pitched at.

Let's examine two concepts, around which most ideas in this book will revolve.

PEOPLE BUY ON EMOTION AND JUSTIFY WITH FACT

Nearly all decisions to buy are based on an emotional reaction, then factual justifications are made. We will tell people we bought a new word processor to improve the efficiency of our office and because it had a fine reliability record. In fact, we bought because a word processor is one hell of a status symbol and the salesperson made us feel bright because we could operate it.

We just bought a new home. Why? Does it keep out the rain any better than the old one? We tell our friends it is an excellent investment in inflationary times and we needed more room. Actually, we wanted the sort of home that reflects the person we want to become.

Even high tech and other ostensibly objective decisions are ultimately based on an emotional reaction. Say a purchasing agent is evaluating proposals to provide 10,000 doogers to his firm. The unit price spread from top to bottom is only 1.2 cents. Will the decision to purchase be based on fact? In a sense, yes, but ultimately—no. What will go through the agent's mind is that if he makes a good decision, his continued employment will be assured and his kids can remain in private schools. A bad decision increases the likelihood of a career adjustment interview with the boss. At its deepest level, the decision is emotional.

PEOPLE BUY FOR THEIR REASONS, NOT OURS

No matter how good my reasons may be for you to take a particular course of action, you will decide for your reasons, no matter how dumb they may seem to me.

I should buy a computer with 64,000 bytes of random access memory, or at least the salesperson thinks so. He told me so in his canned pitch. I buy one in a soft desert tan that nicely matches my office decor. You say, "That's stupid." I say you are probably right, but whose money is it anyhow?

I'm transferred to Elephant's Breath, Iowa, and need to buy a home. One of the first questions asked by the Realtor, because she went to Realtors' school, is "How large is your family?"

I reply, "Oh, they're big suckers—must average 200 pounds."

The Realtor says: "No, what I mean is, do you have school-age children?"

"Yes, three."

"Then you'll be delighted to know about our school system here in Elephant's Breath. Our schools are scholastically top-rated in the Midwest and blah, blah, blah, blah. . . ."

What the Realtor doesn't know about me is I *Won't* be delighted to know about the school system. I've been very broke in the past, at which times my kids went to bad schools. They learned something. It's my belief that the principal responsibility for learning lies not with the schools but rather with the student. I further feel the primary function of schools is to keep kids dry in the winter, so they don't get sick. All I want to know about the school is, "Do they leak?"

The Realtor thinks this is the most anti-American, perverted point of view she has ever heard, and so attempts to further enlighten me on the value of education, boring me to death in the process, because I *Should* care about schools. If you bore me, I will not give you my money.

PEOPLE BUY ON EMOTION AND JUSTIFY WITH FACT.

PEOPLE BUY FOR THEIR REASONS, NOT OURS.

I

Getting Somebody
To Sell To

1
THINGS MOTHER NEVER TOLD ME

*"I'm a self-made man, but I think if I had to do
it over again, I'd call in someone else."*

—Rolland Young

I got my first selling job in the early 1960s. I was living in Seattle and had four children, which proved I knew how to do *something*. I had eight dollars, which proved I didn't know much. I had tried to get a job driving a truck for the Home Laundry Company, but they wouldn't hire me. They said I was too volatile and unstable to drive a truck . . . and I felt inadequate.

I decided my career path probably lay in the direction of driving a cab, so I took five of my last eight dollars, went to the Seattle city hall, took the cab drivers' license test—and flunked it . . . and I felt inadequate.

I don't know if you've ever been "not eating broke," but if you have, you know all about garage sales. When you get "not eating broke," you sell off all possessions not absolutely essential for the continuance of vital functions. I'd sold my rifle, hocked my watch and shotgun, and was down to my last fun toy—my bicycle. It had no seat and no handlebars. It was perfectly suited for those people who have lost their ass and don't know which way to turn.

Since I was too lazy to work and too nervous to steal, I thought I'd try selling. I answered an ad in the *Seattle Post Intelligencer* for a salesman. The ad promised to train you to be a professional salesman and a "tiger closer." "*Oh, good,*" I thought. "Maybe they'll teach me sales psychology so I can understand how people think and how they feel inside, so I can take their money."

My interview lasted less than five minutes. They were *so* glad to see me. I had a good, firm pulse and was relatively coherent, so they hired me right off. I was so delighted to be wanted, I didn't even puzzle over the name of this fine, reputable firm. It was Seattle's First Repo Depo. It was a "system" used car operation, the meanest, hardest kind of selling ever to come down the pike.

Peter Kalomiros was my first crew chief, the man who was to train me to become a professional salesman. He brushed his hair with buttered toast. He wore Edwardian-cut plum-colored velvet suits and yellow alligator shoes, just a little run over at the heels. I knew Peter for over three years and never saw his eyes. He always wore wrap-around dark glasses, calling them shades. Peter maintained that people should never see your eyes, as the eyes are the window to the soul. His soul was *black*.

Peter took me to my first sales seminar. I sat right down front, where I could get sweat on, as I didn't want to miss anything. The fellow running the seminar was J. Douglas Edwards, and he was wonderful. He was aggressive, dynamic, hard-charging, and in total command. All those things I was not. In fact, he was so good that he made me feel

4

terrible, because I knew I couldn't do all the things he said I should do . . . and I felt inadequate.

Mr. Edwards said that master salesmen have 75 closes committed by rote and could close customers from sunup in the morning until sundown at night and never repeat the same close twice. Then he talked about guys like me. I had two closes. The first one was, "Well folks, what do you think?" If that didn't get 'em—if they didn't try to wrest my pen from me to sign the order—I'd pull out my big gun backup. I'd look forlornly at them and say, "How about it?"

Mr. Edwards said to have a positive attitude, and I did. I was *positive* I could never learn 75 closes and would, therefore, never be a master salesman . . . and I felt inadequate.

Mr. Edwards said that the way to become really good at selling was to find someone who was already good and then do everything he did. They called this modeling, and that's the way they trained then.

My model was Peter Kalomiros, so I got a jar of Brylcreem and some shades. Now, I've worn heavy prescription lenses since I was four and couldn't afford prescription sunglasses, so I went to Woolworth's and got some regular sunglasses to wear over my prescription lenses. Some folks thought that looked a little odd. The first week I had them on, I fell down the stairs of the office three times and walked into a lot of open car doors, but I felt they made me more like Peter. Nonetheless, I felt inadequate.

Peter ate breakfast. I've always hated breakfast. The mere idea of putting fuel in a cold furnace is repugnant to me. Imagine, eating on an empty stomach. Every morning Peter went to a little greasy spoon two blocks down the street and ate two eggs (good God, they're *unborn animals*), two country sausage patties, hash brown potatoes, and whole wheat toast. Every morning I went with him, ate two eggs (gag), two country sausage patties, hash brown potatoes, and whole wheat toast. In only six months, I gained twenty-four pounds and didn't sell a damn bit better . . . and I felt inadequate.

Here's a concept I want to give you. You are a unique individual, and that uniqueness is your *biggest asset in selling*. The special blend of genes and chromosomes that go to make up you, cannot be duplicated. There has never been, nor will there ever be again, another you. Nowhere else can I go and get that special blend of attitudes, feelings, experiences, and services that I get with *you*.

If we are in agreement that your biggest asset in selling is your uniqueness, here's the problem. The more you try to become like someone else, the less you become like you. This diminishes your biggest asset, your uniqueness.

No one in the world can do a better job of being you than *you*. In your quest for "self-improvement," never lose sight of who you are, or try too hard to change to measure up to other people's perceptions of who you ought to be. When trying to improve your performance, concentrate on your strengths, and to hell with worrying about weaknesses.

Dr. William Glasser, in his book *Schools Without Failure*, sets forth the theory that we fail primarily because we try to do things at which we are no good. If all the little devil wants to do is weave baskets, let him weave baskets until he's good at it. Then confidence will allow him to progress to other fields.

We all have dimples and warts. Many "self-improvement programs" focus on wart removal. Pass on that, and get your dimples going strong. Do things with which you feel comfortable and which you do well, and maybe you'll never have to say, "And I felt inadequate."

2
SELLING OR CLERKING?

"A gossip is one who talks to you about others:
A bore is one who talks to you about himself:
And a brilliant conversationalist is one who talks
to you about yourself.

—*Lisa Kirk*

Selling was once defined as a process whereby the salesperson goes out and surprises the customer. When the customer comes in to surprise the salesperson, it's called
clerking.

Sales trainers, including myself, place much emphasis on
the value of a planned presentation, correct probing, demonstration of benefits, and esoteric closing strategies. The
distinct possibility that our motivation arises from a desire
for profit is certainly worthy of consideration. After all, if
we trainers simply said that selling was a matter of asking
people to buy until somebody does, you wouldn't attend our
seminars, or buy our books and tapes. The truth, however,

is that many people make a fine living doing just that—asking for sales.

People new to selling tend to study sales psychology, methods of presentation, and closing techniques to excess, while ignoring prospecting. This strikes me as being like the guy who mastered ninety-nine ways to make love and didn't have a girl.

Prospecting, in my opinion, is well over half the game in selling. I'm convinced that if you took a five-pound bag of stale Meadow Muffins and stood on a corner, asking all who passed, "You don't want to buy these, do you?", someone would before the sun set.

Another agreeable aspect of being a good prospector is that you get to work with nicer people. Let's face it, some folks are simply not nice. That's the problem with being a manager. You are, by and large, stuck with what you've got. If the people with whom you work are not nice to you, you have to make do, as best you can, and try to get along with them. If you're a good prospector and your customers are less than nice, you can say "To hell with 'em" and go find customers more to your liking. No one should have to go through life dealing with nasty people. Become an excellent prospector and you're sure to find some pleasant ones.

CLERKING

Let's put aside for a moment the joys of prospecting, and discuss "clerking": the handling of customers who come in and surprise you. Your objectives would include:

1. Developing rapport

2. Understanding the customer's needs
3. Determining the customer's ability to buy (qualifying)

Fortunately, all three objectives can be achieved by asking questions. There are few statements of fact which cannot easily be converted to questions and be more readily accepted.

Questions, or probes, are divided into two categories, nondirective and directive.

Nondirective Probes

These are questions which cannot be answered "yes" or "no" and which allow the customer to fully explain what is on his mind. They have also been called "open questions," among other things. Nondirective probes often, but not always, start with one of these six words:

WHO
WHAT
WHEN
WHY
WHERE
HOW

Rudyard Kipling called these his "Six Honest Serving Men, Who Taught Me All I Know."

Nondirective probes not only will help you to achieve the second and third objectives, but will do more than anything else to help you achieve rapport. I know of no finer way of gaining people's affection than to listen to them talk about that which interests them most: Themselves.

A number of years ago, in my dark, divorced days, I was

conducting a seminar at the Newporter Hotel, in Newport Beach, California. I had been introduced to a lovely young woman who agreed to have dinner with me, which was good, as she had a car.

She picked me up at the hotel. Almost as soon as I got in her car, she said: "Hank, I don't know much about you. What do you do for a living?"

I said: "I'm a real estate broker."

She said: "I'd hate to impose on your time off and ask you to talk shop, but I've always been fascinated by real estate and know no one in the field. Would you tell me a little about real estate?"

Would I? "Blah, blah, blah, blah." I told her about alluvion, avulsion, and accretion. I told her how many members sat on the real estate commission. I told her about guaranteed loans, insured loans, variable interest rates, and graduated payment trust deeds. I taught her how to read mortgage yield tables. I told her more about real estate than I knew. She was not only intelligent and perceptive, she was undoubtedly one of the finest conversationalists I had ever met.

She said, "*What* brings you to Newport Beach?"

I said, "I'm down here for a real estate seminar."

She said, "Isn't that admirable. With all you obviously know about real estate, you're still taking seminars to keep up with the latest developments."

I said, "No, no. I'm not taking the seminar, I'm *giving* the seminar."

She said, "Isn't that *wonderful*. It would terrify me to speak before a group. *How* did you overcome stage fright?"

Me: "Blah, blah, blah, blah." I told her about every talk I'd made since the age of two. She listened intently and with obvious interest for over an hour and a half. I determined she was not only intelligent, perceptive, and a fine conversationalist; she was getting taller and thinner, too.

She: *"When* you're not selling real estate or conducting seminars, *what* do you do to relax?"

Me: "Well, I play tennis and racquetball, I go bicycle-riding, and I'm a scuba diver."

She: "A scuba diver. Isn't that awfully dangerous?"

Me: "Well, there is a certain element of risk, but if you're brave. . . ."

She: *"What* would you do if you saw a shark?"

Me: "Blah, blah, blah, blah." I told her about gray sharks, white sharks, blue sharks, tipped sharks, tiger sharks, hammerhead sharks, nurse sharks, white sharks, seals, sea lions, and sea otters. I told her about a rogue abalone that tried to get my glove. I taught her how to read the navy decompression tables.

By the time we had finished dinner and a half dozen rusty nails, I was ready to make a lifetime commitment. I was in love. (Couldn't remember her name, though.) Through the adroit use of nondirective probes, she had really done a selling job. She had developed rapport beyond all belief. She had a clear understanding of my needs, chief among which was the need to be listened to, and had convinced me to buy dinner and almost anything else her heart desired.

I submit to you that we need to employ the very same process when a customer comes in to surprise us. We need to have questions to ask that will accomplish our objectives in a low-key, friendly, nonthreatening way.

REAL ESTATE EXAMPLES

1. *Where* are you living now?
2. *What* do you most like about your present home?

3. *What* do you most want in your new home?
4. *How* soon must you move?
5. *How* long have you been looking?
6. *When* you find the house you seek, do you plan to pay all cash?
7. *What* are your plans to finance?
8. *Why* are you moving?
9. *Who* else will be involved in the decision to buy?
10. *When* can you go see a home?

AUTOMOBILE EXAMPLES

1. *What* brought you in to see us?
2. *What* kind of car are you now driving?
3. *Who* else will be driving the car?
4. *When* would you like delivery?
5. *How* important is (gas mileage, luxury, speed, styling) to you?
6. *How* much is owed on your present car?
7. *When* you decide on a car, do you plan to pay cash?
8. *Why* did you buy your present car?
9. *When* can we go for a short ride in a_____?
10. *What* color do you like best?

RETAIL EXAMPLES

1. *What* are you looking for?
2. *Who* will be using it?
3. *How* many other items of this type have you seen?
4. *How* did you feel about them?
5. *When* do you plan to buy?
6. *How* important is quality to you?

7. *How* soon do you need delivery?
8. *What* size do you wear?
9. *Where* else have you been looking?
10. *Why* not take it with you right now?

I'm sure you get the drift. As we'll discuss, it isn't so important which words you use. What matters is that they be phrased as questions and that you know what to ask.

Directive Probes

These are questions that can often, but not always, be answered "yes" or "no." They are used to direct the conversation to areas that you feel need to be addressed. They are also very useful when a Nondirective probe fails to produce the desired results. Some examples:

> Salesperson: *"What* do you most want in your new home?"
> Customer: "I'm not sure, we want a lot of things."
> Salesperson: "Are schools important to you?"
>
> Salesperson: *Why* did you buy your present car?
> Customer: "Beats the hell out of me."
> Salesperson: "Was the gas mileage a primary consideration?"
>
> Salesperson: *"What* are you looking for?"
> Customer: "I'm just looking."
> Salesperson: "We have a special value on blue doogers today. What size would you need?"

As we progress together, we'll talk a lot more about probes, as they are the foundation on which today's selling is based.

THE 80–20 RULE OF SELLING

I'm going to propose to you the *80–20 rule of selling*. Which means, the customer talks 80 percent of the time and we talk 20 percent. When we talk, we ask questions to cause the customer to talk more. He who talks dominates the conversation; he who listens controls it.

Now your assignment, should you choose to accept it, is to list at least ten questions you can ask next time a customer comes in and surprises *You*:

1. _____

2. _____

3. _____

4. _____

5. _____

6. _____

7. _____

8. _____

9. _____

10. _____

3
I READ YOU LOUD AND CLEAR

"I don't care how much a man talks, if he only says it in a few words."

—Josh Billings

Early in the history of sales training, people used to key in on the top salesman (yes, they were largely men then), find out what they were saying to customers, and then teach the pitch, verbatim, to all the lesser mortals. It didn't work terribly well, but halitosis is better than no breath at all, so they did it that way.

Some of these early sales giants then became sales trainers and slightly modified the approach. They stopped telling people what they actually said and did, and started telling people what they thought they *should have said and done.* This sounded a whole lot better and therefore sold well, but was actually a huge step away from reality in sales training.

Trainers developed a whole vocabulary of "good" selling

words and "bad" selling words. You should never say "sign," always say "approve" or "O.K." You should never say "deal," always say "transaction." You should never say "contract," always say "paperwork." Well, I went to a lot of seminars and really bought into this line of thinking. Instead of saying "How much money are you able to put down?", I learned to say "What portion of your savings have you set aside for your initial investment?"

My vocabulary transformation wasn't easy. These mouthfuls were hard to learn and hard to say clearly. My tongue kept getting twisted, but I kept at it and learned. After I got over the initial discomfort of unfamiliar phrases, I began paying attention to the reactions of my customers.

I'd say, "Tell me, Mr. and Mrs. Gorfman, what portion of your savings have you set aside for your initial investment?"

They'd look at each other blankly, then look at me and chime, in unison, "Huh?"

Then I'd have to say, "How many bucks you got to put down on this shack, Jack?"

They'd say, "Oh, we've got $15,000 counting money, marbles, and chalk."

Effective communication had been restored. It occurred to me that if I was going to have to get basic eventually, the longer I took to get basic, the more likely were we to have a complete communication breakdown.

It further occurred to me that if my objective was to create an open, honest, intimate relationship with my buyers, fancy words might give the impression I was slick and sneaky. This was totally counterproductive to my objectives. I began to relearn a whole new vocabulary of direct communication.

When trained as new salespeople, we tend to spend 90 percent of our time learning the jargon and "canned pitches" associated with our chosen field. This is the way it's always been done.

But here comes Dr. Albert Mehrabian of the University of Southern California to knock our whole theory into a cocked hat. His studies indicate that, when we seek to communicate thoughts, ideas, feelings, and attitudes to other people, only 7 percent of their reaction will stem from the words we use. *Only 7 percent?* You mean we've been spending 90 percent of our time and effort learning that which is only 7 percent effective?

Absolutely. Ain't that the pits? Dr. Mehrabian finds that people form opinions and perceptions about us and what we say on this basis:

- 7% verbal (the *words* we use)
- 38% vocal (how we *sound* when we say what we say)
- 55% Nonverbal (how we *look* when we say what we say)

This may make word selection seem unimportant. But let's look at selling today. The competition is tough, so I don't want to be at even a 7 percent disadvantage. That's often enough to tip the scales against us.

DESCRIPTIVE WORDS

As noted before, people buy on emotion and justify with fact. We are not car salespeople, or Realtors, or insurance folks, or dooger peddlers, we're *dream merchants*. We don't sell products or services, we sell the benefits these products or services will provide to our customers. We need to generate an emotional reaction, and descriptive words are a wonderful ally.

Average auto salesperson: "This car is aerodynamically designed for maximum fuel efficiency."

Superior auto salesperson: "Can't you just see the expressions on the faces of your friends and neighbors when you pull up in this low-slung, sleek beauty?"

Average real estate salesperson: "The home has a lovely view."

Superior real estate salesperson: "Can you imagine sitting on this veranda on a soft summer evening, a breeze whispering through the pines, watching the sun turn blood red as it dips behind the hills?"

Average insurance salesperson: "This whole life policy has the best rates in the industry."

Superior insurance salesperson: "I'll bet you'd sleep a lot easier knowing that whatever happens to you, Freddie's college education is assured. He'll look so handsome, marching proudly up to get his diploma."

Average dooger peddler: "Our quality control assures less than 3 percent rejects."

Superior dooger salesperson: "You'll be the hero of sales and marketing because of your on-time delivery. Our 97 percent acceptance rate assures it. Wouldn't it feel great to stop all those rude calls from sales, to walk into the company lunchroom, head held high?"

Yes, even the most technical of products are purchased on emotion and justified with fact. Think about the emotional reaction you want to generate, then select appropriate terminology.

Nerve Words

We are all individuals. One thing of which you can be absolutely certain is that every person you meet is different from every other person you have ever met. We differ not only genetically, but experientially. People's reactions to you will differ widely, depending on their experiences, environment, and personality.

Enter nerve words. These are words that create a gut-level, emotional reaction, usually negative, on the part of the receiver. These words vary widely from person to person, from time to time, and from area to area.

Today we all hear words on TV that we wouldn't have heard at cocktail parties twenty years ago. And the reverse is also true. Take the word "Jap." This is not readily accepted in polite society today, yet in 1940 the term was on the front page of every newspaper in the country.

The word "bum" in this country is synonymous with hobo or tramp—completely acceptable. In Australia, it is used to describe the posterior and is certain to bring about startled glances when applied to another person, as I once found to my consternation.

Nerve words should generally be avoided, as they may bring about an early end to the sales presentation. Real profanity or scatological terms are nearly guaranteed to lose you points.

If you do use a potential nerve word, eye contact is one of the better ways to ascertain how it's being received. If you're chatting along and suddenly your receiver's eyes snap into sharp focus, or dart about nervously, you may have hit a nerve word. Best not to say it again, unless you want to provoke a similar or more violent reaction.

Nerve words should generally be avoided, *unless you perceive your receiver is apathetic.* If you see that your listener's eyes have gone out of focus, and especially if he seems on the verge of dozing off, you might consider hitting him with a nerve word. Like "sperm." This is virtually guaranteed to restore the focus of attention to you.

Clearly, nerve words are to be used sparingly, and only between consenting adults.

Technical Data

People buy on emotion. The problem is that technical data have never been known to generate much of an emotional reaction, except among an obscure cult of nuclear physicists living in the Mojave Desert.

Buyers will use technical data to disqualify you as a supplier, or to justify why they bought or did not buy, but they seldom really buy because of such data.

The ad says the home has 2,400 square feet. The ad writer wrote that because he thought 2,400 square feet was big. Yet consider a reader of the ad who is living in a 2,600-square-foot home and decides not to look at the house—a house that might have served her family well. Had the writer substituted "massive" or "spacious" for technical data, a buyer, a seller, and a real estate person might all be happier.

The auto salesperson says, "This trunk holds 13.2 cubic feet." The buyer dozes off. A more favorable response might be produced by: "The trunk will hold all your luggage for a weekend trip, keeping the bags out of the back seat. Wouldn't that reduce the whining level of your children?"

There is a saying, "What we say or write is not important. What is important is what goes on in the mind of the decoder *about* what we say or write."

Technical data should only be used to support an emotional reaction and should *always* be linked to a benefit for the buyer.

Semantics

The English language is currently composed of about 150,000 words and is growing and changing daily. The people who sell *21 Days to a Better Vocabulary*, and like tomes, would have us believe that our command of the language is a measure of how civilized we are. They may be right, but let's look for a minute at the receivers of what we say.

Each of us has two kinds of vocabularies: active and passive. Our active vocabulary is comprised of words that we can define, that we clearly understand, and that, left to our own devices, we would use in daily conversation. The average American's active vocabulary contains about *3,500 words*.

Our passive vocabulary is comprised of words we cannot define, don't clearly understand, and, left to our own devices, would not normally use in daily conversation. However, when these words appear in context with words from our active vocabulary, we roughly catch the meaning. The average American's passive vocabulary contains about *7,000 words*. When was the last time you looked up a word in the dictionary? Pollsters tell us that over 40 percent of adult Americans have not opened a dictionary since achieving adulthood.

We have over 150,000 words at our command to facilitate communication with other people, but our average receiver only understands 10,500 of them, at best. As George Du Murier says:

> Language is a poor thing. You fill your lungs with wind and shake a little slit in your throat and make mouths and that shakes the air; and the air shakes a pair of little drums in my head . . . and my brain seizes your meaning in the rough. What a roundabout way and what a waste of time.

A well-developed vocabulary is not only nonessential for success in selling, it may actually be counterproductive if used injudiciously. Many fine salespeople have performed beautifully with the most meager of formal educations, because they related well to *people*.

I've always loved the tale of the startled sales manager who received this report from the field:

"Deer Boss: I seen this outfit which they ain't never baut a dimes worth of nothing from us and I sole them a couple hundred thousand dollars worth of guds. On to Chawgo."

Two days later, from "Chawgo," came another report: "I cum here and sole them a half milyon. . . ."

Both letters were posted on the company's bulletin board, with a note appended by the outfit's president: "We've been spendin too much time hear trying to spel, instead of trying to sel. Let's watch those sails. I want everybody should read these letters from Gooch who is on the rode doin a grate job for us, and you should go out and do like he done."

38 PERCENT VOCAL

As we saw, people will make decisions about us based almost 40 percent not on what we say but on how we sound when we say it. Men, particularly, prove that in daily conversation. They may say the most atrocious things to one another, but in a friendly tone of voice. Raucous laughs ensue, and a good time is had by all. If the very same words were spoken sans the laughs and friendly voice tone, many of the participants would take their teeth home in a bag.

Obviously, then, in attempting to establish clear communication with people, a good voice is a decided asset. Here's the problem. I'm not sure how you get a good voice. Oh, I know one when I hear one, but it's tough to tell someone in print how to develop a good voice. I do, however, know something of nearly equal value. I know what makes up a *bad* voice and ways in which you can avoid having one, which brings you closer to a good voice.

Let's examine the various qualities that go to make up a voice.

Enunciation

Enunciation is the clarity with which we pronounce our words. For years, public speakers have been telling us we must pronounce each word clearly and roundly so that none of our meaning will be lost. This may be just dandy in front of 2,000 people, but it sure sounds funny in the coffee shop, where some of the trainees continue to e—nun—ci—ate.

Enunciation that is overly clear and precise may convey condescension, insincerity, or even annoyance. Have you ever noticed how clearly you can enunciate when you are annoyed?

Since, in all probability, none of these are attitudes we really want to convey to our receivers, I'm going to advise that you *not* enunciate to excess in daily conversation. Now, I'm not suggesting you mumble like Marlon Brando, but rather smooth the edges off the words to create a softness. Don't worry about your meaning being lost; we've just shown that most people probably don't understand half of the words you use anyhow.

Inflection

The way we place em*pha*sis on various syl*la*bles will have a great deal to do with the message actually received by our decoder. Let's take the simple sentence "I did not say he beats his wife" and get seven different meanings from it, merely by moving the emphasis from word to word.

Below, the words to be stressed are in italics. Read each sentence aloud, with the stress, and see if you agree with the connotation that follows.

"*I* did not say he beats his wife."
Someone else has been saying he beats his wife.

"I did *not* say he beats his wife."
The word is out on the street, but it didn't come from me.

"I did not *say* he beats his wife."
I have my own private thoughts which may, or may not, include his physical pursuits, but I didn't voice them.

"I did not say *he* beats his wife."
Wife beating is a common occurrence in my circle of acquaintances, but he is not necessarily a participant therein.

"I did not say he *beats* his wife."
He is intimately familiar with various methods of physical and psychological degradation, but beating is not his thing. It leaves marks.

"I did not say he beats *his* wife."
That's the last time I'm taking *my* wife to his house for dinner.

"I did not say he beats his *wife*."
His children, furniture, and household pets are in advanced stages of disrepair, but his wife is quite well, thank you.

As we've seen, inflection can change the entire meaning of your conversation. At least as bad as misplaced inflection is no inflection at all. This will cause your listeners to doze off in seconds flat.

It might be a good idea to record some of your conversations to hear what your receivers hear. Our inflection deserves special attention.

Pitch

Did you ever listen to Edith Bunker on the TV series *All in the Family*? Does she sound like the all-time dingbat? If you had a million-dollar inheritance, would you seek Edith to manage it for you? Yet, if you listen to Jean Stapleton, who played Edith, in a personal interview, you'll notice her normal voice is nearly two octaves below that of Edith. Does this mean she has purposely raised the pitch of her voice to create the impression that she doesn't have both oars in the water? You've got it.

Our society equates a deep voice, male or female, with credibility. As I'm writing this, the most believed man in America is Walter Cronkite, even though he's retired. More people believe Walter Cronkite than any other human being. Does he have a deep voice? When Walter says, "And that's the way it is," are you inclined to argue?

You may say, "I've always had a high voice. I was born with it and that's just the way I am."

Bull. Your voice is controlled by muscles, and muscles can be trained. Voice coaches have an exercise called humming down. All you do to lower the normal pitch of your voice is, while standing, hum down the scale to the lowest note you can reach and hold it as long as you can. Do this three or four times a day (in private because it looks silly), and *voilà*, a deeper voice. Try it.

Speed

Normal speaking rates tend to run at something less than 200 words per minute, with gusts of up to twice that. When one speaks at the same rate for an extended period, communication suffers.

When we speak rapidly, people view us with a jaundiced eye. Our vernacular even provides for the diminished credibility of rapid speech. "An insurance man came out here and *fast talked* me into a million-dollar policy," complains the fleeced. There is another drawback to being a fast talker: you often say things you haven't thought of yet.

If, on the other hand, you speak constantly in a slow and measured fashion to maximize your credibility, you will often find that many of your listeners have elected to use their faces for paperweights.

The study of neurolinguistic programming may lack empirical data, but some of its concepts are usable in everyday life. One such is that we tend to be drawn to people like ourselves. We like people who speak at the same rate we do. Slow speakers tend to distrust, and become agitated by, fast speakers. Fast talkers tend to become bored, impatient, and irritated by slow talkers. If our objective is to generate affinity, then it would seem prudent to roughly approximate the speech patterns of our listener.

In any event, varying your rate of speech will optimize attention on the part of your listener.

Tone

Barbara Walters is a lovely, intelligent, talented, and highly compensated lady, but she sure isn't paid because of her voice. When you watch and listen to her speak, from whence does her voice seem to emanate? Her nose, right? How Miss Walters arrived at this method of speaking is unclear, but I sometimes wonder if kindergarten wasn't at the root of it. In some kindergartens children are taught to breathe, though it seems they must have had some inkling of the process if they lasted long enough to get to kindergarten. The hapless five-year-olds are lined up and forced to puff up their bony little chests, then chant, in unison, "In goes the good air, *whooosh*, out goes the bad air."

That's all wrong. Now just for fun, poke yourself in the side, under your arm (isn't this fun?). Those hard things, in case you haven't kept up on your physiology, are called ribs. They're put there to keep sharp things out of your thorax, the cavity that contains the heart and lungs. Ribs, unlike your lungs, are relatively inflexible. Your lungs hold about five pints of air, just as you're sitting now. Fully inflated, they'll hold ten pints of air. Fully deflated, they hold two pints. Thus there is an eight-pint, or one-gallon, differential. That's a lot of expansion against relatively inflexible ribs.

Fortunately, the Great Architect provided for this expansion with a lateral membrane called the diaphragm, put there to keep your lungs from falling into the gory stuff. That's a good design. Can you imagine, if your lungs were allowed to fall into the gory stuff, how bad your breath would be?

When you inhale, your lungs should expand down against the diaphragm, expanding the strongest muscles in your body, the abdominal girdle. Then when you exhale, you contract the abdominal girdle and your voice comes out deep and strong, rather than thin and reedy.

Next time you go to an opera, watch the basso profundo's tummy. When he's going to go for a big one, it'll expand seven or eight inches. Then when he pulls it in, he'll blow out streetlights.

Volume

It has been said that a good argument is not necessarily a loud one. Yet I daily see salespeople practically yelling at their customers. Obviously, we have to speak loudly enough to be heard, but excessive volume indicates, and provokes, stress and fear. If we raise our voices at our customers, we'll demonstrate nervousness, overeagerness, or so much pressuring that we'll scare them. On the other hand, next time you really want to make a salient point, *whisper*. Notice how, when someone whispers, everyone listens? That's because the only reason you could have for whispering is because you have *secret information*. And nobody wants to miss out on secret information.

The proper blending of all the voice characteristics that have been discussed will result in a *warm* voice. A warm voice is a great asset in selling.

55 PERCENT NONVERBAL

Over half of our ability to effectively communicate ideas, thoughts, feelings, and attitudes to people is based not on what we say, not on how we sound when we say it, but how we *look* when we say it. You have, at your command, the most remarkable communication device ever known to man. It's the large device on the front of your head, called your face.

Your face is as unique as you are. No other face exactly like yours has ever been, or ever again will be, built. You are a "one off" model. Since your face is as individual as your fingerprint, some government scientists, working with your tax dollars, came up with a bright idea. Shoot your face with a TV camera and store your image in a computer bank. Then when you want to get in to see the secret stuff, the computer would compare your TV image with that stored in the data bank and say, "O.K., you're one of the good guys. Come in and look at the secret stuff." Great idea. Didn't work.

Your face not only is unique but is never the same twice. The only computer sufficiently complex to be able to recognize you, with your myriad expressions, is another human brain.

If indeed your objective is to communicate with maximum effectiveness, remove all impediments to that objective.

I submit to you that shaded or tinted glasses obscure your eyes and therefore should never be worn while selling. There is, in fact, a school of thought which prefers contact lenses to spectacles. Not for reasons of vanity, but for clarity of communication.

In recent years, moustaches and even full beards have been gaining favor. I think they are stylish, distinguished, and dashing. I have noticed, however, that at over five paces, it's very difficult to tell whether a beard is smiling, leering, or frowning. Fur is, by and large, fur.

I would never be so presumptuous as to try to dictate matters of personal taste; it wouldn't do any good anyhow. I would, however, suggest that you be intensely aware of the communication value of your face and carefully evaluate anything that impedes its function.

Moving downward, in normal business situations over 95 percent of our bodies are covered by clothes. The clothes we wear make a strong nonverbal statement about us. Salespeople for years have told me that they fear dressing too well, as their customers might think they are making too much money. *Bull.* Do you like to do business with a loser? Neither do most people.

A fine rule is to "dress like the people your customers go to for advice." High-quality, well-coordinated clothes not only make you look better, they make you *feel* better as well. I submit that you are much better off with fewer clothes but ones of very high quality and conservative construction. Such clothes wear longer too.

Fifty-five percent of your impact on people is visual. Do all in your power to be certain that the *you* they see is the best you that you can be. You never get a second chance to make a first impression.

4
ASK NOT FOR WHOM THE BELL TOLLS. . . .
OR, THE TELEPHONE (WOO-WOO) SURPRISE

*"Poverty is no disgrace to a man, but it is
confoundedly inconvenient."*

—*Sydney Smith*

Among the most disconcerting of the events in a salesperson's day is when a customer surprises you on the telephone. You don't even get to see him coming.

Let's first review some things you have probably already been told, through previous telephone training.

1. Be prepared. Know your inventory. Know the benefits of your product or service. Have all necessary information at your fingertips.

31

2. Have a positive attitude. Feel good about yourself, your company, your product, and your customer.
3. Smile. A smile will be reflected in your voice. Put a little mirror on your desk, so you can watch yourself smile.
4. Exude confidence. Speak slowly, low, and distinctly. Your stability and credibility will be automatically conveyed to your customer.

Bull. On a given day, if you do nothing but sit around your office, waiting for someone to call you, you're going to go broke. You are going to have to be busy with other activities, which means that, of necessity, you are going to be less than ready when the phone rings.

Let's talk about the real world. The world of hangovers and blackheads. Yes, that's right, we all have those days. "Positive thinkers" have been telling us for years that every day must be a *good* day. As a result, when we have a bad day, we feel terrible—we berate ourselves for being "negative" and therefore abnormal. This makes a bad day even worse.

I don't know about your life, but in mine, not all days are so hot. Only a mediocre person is always at his best. I have days when it takes everything I've got just to keep up with the losers. My observations indicate that if you can get about three out of ten really good days, you're doing better than most folks. Some days you wrestle the bear, some days the bear wrestles you. That's just the way it is in the real world.

We don't need methods to try to become silver-tongued superstars; we need methods to help us perform adequately, even when we don't feel like it. There is no disgrace in falling down, only in staying down. Charles Kettering, the inventor of the Overhead Valve V-8 engine, among

32

other things, said: "The only time you must not fail is the last time you try."

Let's get matters in proper perspective. Some days are for living, others are for getting through. The next time David Hartman leers out of your TV at 8:00 A.M. and commands you to *"Go out and make it a good day!"* you tell him, "Bunch it, David. I'll do the best I can with little bitty tools." You won't hurt David's feelings and you'll be better for it.

Let's examine a typical day on which you might receive an ad call. You're sitting at your workplace at 10:00 A.M., not hurting anybody. Your banker has just called to tell you your note's due in a week. He wants to know how you're going to pay it. *He* wants to know? The big deal you've been working on for thirteen months (you've carried that turkey longer than its mother did) just blew up. You have a cold coming on, and you're sure your tonsils are red and sore as a boil. A pimple's beginning to form between your eyes. At home last night, the school called about little Harvey, your only son, the light of your life. He's been wearing dresses again.

Now, the phone rings and the voice on the other end says, "I'm calling about your ad in the paper."

You think: "Ad?? OhmiGod, why would we have an ad? We already sold all our stuff—I think." You find yourself, mired irretrievably, dead smack in the middle of a mental cul-de-sac. Right now the most creative thing it's possible for you to do is slop coffee all over your desk. If you are not so totally gripped by panic that you are completely mute, you will probably begin to babble incoherently, yet quickly. Your voice rises as your speed increases, words tumbling over one another—yet you press onward, as silence would be deafening. In less than ninety seconds, you tell *all* you know about everything, which today is unlikely to be much. The customer thanks you and hangs up, never to be heard from again.

Sound familiar? It happens in sales organizations, all over the world, every day. So what can be done about it?

THE CALLER'S OBJECTIVES

Every time a customer calls your place of business, he operates on a hidden agenda. He has a set of objectives, partially buried in his unconscious mind, that he is hell bent to fulfill. Just because he is unaware, at the conscious level, of many of those objectives does not mean they are non-existent. They guide the caller's behavior as clearly as our objectives guide our behavior.

Often the caller's objectives are ranked like this:

1. To Buy Something

Salespeople all over the world tell me, "I don't need to get better on the phone. Nobody but flakes call us anyhow." *Bull.* Calling around on the phone is not a lot of fun. Most people would as soon go to the dentist as call strangers. When you get a request for information on the phone, it's a pretty reliable indicator of a high level of motivation on the part of the caller. There's a good chance he'll buy unless we get in the way of the sale.

2. To Eliminate You

Look at the process we all go through in reading ads, deciding which ones to call about. "No, that's too expensive." "No, that's too small." "No, that's in the wrong area." "No, George had one of those and it broke in less than a month."

We attempt to continue this process when we pick up the phone. We want to try to get the salesperson to say something that will help us blow him out of the water, thereby narrowing our buying alternatives and making our purchase decision easier.

3. To Gain Information

In order to help us eliminate the salesperson, we need information. The more information we get, the easier it is to eliminate the salesperson. It has been said, and I believe, that: "A closed mouth gathers no foot." The less we talk, the more effective we'll be. Remember, he who talks *Dominates* the conversation. He who listens *Controls* the conversation.

4. To Avoid Involvement

Sometimes we are less than wildly excited about getting in the presence of a salesperson, as our experience with salespeople in the past has been other than totally enjoyable. Possibly we've been ignored or treated shabbily. Worse yet, we may have been high-pressured or pitched at. Ira Hayes says, "The only thing we've got holding down inflation in this country is lousy service. We'd all buy lots more if we could just get waited on."

If our perception of salespeople in general is that they're not fun to be with, we'd have to be a few shingles light of a full load to want to confront one face-to-face. The reality is this: most people don't want to be around you because of their past associations with salespeople. They'd rather call.

Well now, if the caller is going to operate from a hidden agenda, containing objectives to guide his behavior, wouldn't we be at a distinct disadvantage if we had no objectives ourselves? Surely.

OUR OBJECTIVES

Objective No. 1 is to *get an appointment.*

Some folks, in limited types of selling (magazines, donations, etc.), claim they can sell on the phone. This has never worked very well for me. I have trouble closing a deal on the phone. We have not yet devised a way to get a pen to pass through that curly section of the phone cord and apply itself to a purchase contract.

My personal perception is that the phone is *only* good for making an appointment. We can only sell effectively when we are belly to belly with the buyer. Therefore, all of our efforts should be directed toward getting together with the buyer at the earliest opportunity.

If we had a list of objectives, ranked in declining order of importance from 1 to 10, number 1 is *get an appointment* and the next one is number 10, and there is no 2 through 9.

Objective No. 10 is to *get a valid name and phone number.*

Now forgive me for the way I phrased that, but sometimes in my world, buyers don't give us their real names. On occasion, we've called back a prospective buyer only to get Dial-a-Prayer.

A name and a number are fine and nice to have, if they are real, but they are no substitute for an appointment. You can have a truckload of names and numbers, but if you don't get appointments, you don't get to sell your stuff— and selling your stuff is the name of the game.

Selling is communicating. In the process of effective communication, it is far more important to understand than to be understood. We don't need to find ways to outflow more data, but to *inflow* more data. We need to make the 80–20 rule of selling our major strength.

Wouldn't it be terrific if you had a list of questions you could ask of incoming callers, taped to your desk, by your phone? Then when you found yourself in a mental cul-de-sac, you could say, "Oh good, I'll ask them #5." I won't give you the questions I use, because then you'd be trying to use my words in your world and we'd be right back with the old "canned pitch."

Your assignment now, should you choose to accept it, is to make a list of questions, in your words, that would be effective in your world. Questions you can use to bail yourself out when you're in trouble.

Let me give you some criteria, or guidelines, for the questions you are going to generate. We want a list of questions that:

1. GET US INFORMATION

Let's create questions that will help the caller hold up his 80 percent end of the 80–20 rule. We need to get as much information about the caller and his needs as possible. The nondirective, or open, questions are very effective here.

2. LEAD TO AN APPOINTMENT

We get appointments by being the sort of person our caller would like to meet. We can develop affinity faster by listening to the caller than by any other method I know.

People will want to meet us *only* if they feel it will benefit them to do so. People make decisions for their reasons, not ours. We can tell them it will be to their benefit, but that doesn't work very well. Instead, let's consider asking them hard questions. Hard questions make the caller aware that we may possess information valuable to him which he does not possess.

Hard questions can often be directive probes, such as: "Have you had your present home appraised?" or "Have you driven a new Slosh Pot 6?" or "What metric size would you wear?" Questions like these make the caller aware that we may have information for him that he needs, without actually telling him so.

Of course, the very best way to get an appointment is to *ask for it*. The more frequently we ask, the more likely we are to get.

3. PERPETUATE THE CONVERSATION

Here the objective is to keep the caller talking until such time as he has agreed to an appointment. Nondirective probes stimulate the greatest amount of conversation on the part of the caller. Since most people will not hang up while they're talking, this will keep us in contact long enough to optimize our opportunity to get an appointment.

4. DISQUALIFY NEITHER THE CUSTOMER NOR THE SALESPERSON

How much money the caller has or how much he earns is not important at this time. We've made a money investment merely to get the customer to call us; let's invest a little time now to capitalize on that investment. If we later find that the caller is not qualified to buy our products, we can always say, *"Don't you ever call this office again."* On the other hand, after a face-to-face conversation, we may find a way for the buyer to buy that was not readily apparent over the phone.

38

I once had a woman named Katherine Neeley selling real estate for me. She was *great* on the phone. She had a big, warm voice—probably because she was a big, warm woman. So big, in fact, that she had more chins than the Hong Kong phone book. People would call in on ads, she'd engage them in conversation, and they'd tell her their most intimate secrets. I've seen her keep people talking on the phone for 45 minutes. She was so good on the phone that we used to tape her and play the tapes at sales meetings.

Despite her talents, in a little over a year with my company, she sold two houses. I determined I could no longer afford the luxury of our mutual association, so we had a career adjustment meeting and I dehired her. In cleaning out her desk, I found, in her upper right-hand drawer, 200 slips of paper. Each one had a name and phone number; she never missed on names and numbers. The slips also had interesting little notations. One said, "Too many children." This might have been a value judgment. One said, "poor credit." How she induced some poor soul to divulge that over the phone I'll never know. But she did it. One note said, "Couldn't buy a painted rock."

By effectively questioning our callers, she had managed to disqualify 200 potential buyers. At the time, calls in response to my ad cost me $30 each to generate. Now I'm no mathematical whiz, but I could multiply $30 by 200 and found that she had $6,000 of my money *in her desk drawer.* I was concerned.

My course of action was clear. I would call all 200 of those prospective buyers, make appointments, and give them to the remaining members of our staff. I'm not that strong. Of the 15 I actually called, 11 had already purchased from someone less particular.

Get them in the office now. You can always run them off later.

Now to your list of questions. The words, and the order in which the questions are asked, are not important, with the exception of the first three questions. Over the years, we've developed three questions which, if asked of an ad caller in this order, will convert over 80 percent of our inquiries to appointments. Below are the questions, along with an examination of what they can hope to accomplish for you.

1. "WILL YOU READ ME THE WHOLE AD, PLEASE?"

This is a terrific opener on an ad call, as it gives you four valuable assets.

Time. You need time to get your ears back on. The phone call startled you and you need to time to remember you're in your office, not in Hawaii where you were daydreaming. While the caller reads the ad, you'll have 90 to 120 seconds to compose yourself and mop the coffee off your papers.

Information. If you listen carefully, callers will tell you plenty about themselves as they read you the ad. You can use this information to more effectively communicate with them. Are they male or female? Do they speak fast or slow? Do they understand and pronounce correctly all the words they read?

Practice Listening. We all talk a lot when in our workplace. We're among friends and conversation comes easily, so we just run our mouths perpetually. Now it's time to sell, and talking is inappropriate. We'll have 90 to 120 seconds to see how well we can shut up. Let's resist all temptation to help the caller read the ad, although we know it by heart. Let the customer be the star in this recitation.

Control. Here's a basic fact in selling. People will do business with you in direct proportion to the degree to which they become psychologically dependent on you. Another term for psychological dependency is control. If folks become accustomed to doing what you tell them to do, it's not hard for them to sign a contract when you say, "Press hard, the fourth copy's yours."

That control doesn't just happen. It is layered in in small doses which begin at the first ringing of the phone.

SAMPLE

> HE: "Hi. I'm calling about your ad in the paper."
> WE: "Wonderful. *Will you read me the whole ad, please?*"
> HE: "Yeah. It says 'Sloshpot 6 only $12,000.' "
> WE: "Yes, go on."
> HE: "You mean the *whole* ad?"
> WE: "Yes, we have several ads running and I want to be sure we have the right one. Please read me the whole ad."

And they'll do it. They want the information, so they'll read you the whole ad. And you'll have taken the first small step toward getting control.

2. "WHAT SPECIFICALLY ABOUT THAT AD ATTRACTED YOUR CALL?"

Each of our ads will normally contain over five feature benefits. People are usually motivated to call by only one or two of them, but we don't know which one or two. People buy for their reasons, not ours.

Our ad said:

> Sloshpot 6
> Only $12,000
> Automatic transmission

Runs on gas/diesel
Power steering
Power windows
Power door locks
High-compression hubcaps
Anatomically designed seats
Sunroof
Don't Delay—Call Today   555-1212

Maybe this buyer is calling because Dad always drove a Sloshpot and loved them. He'd have bought one before if only they'd had power door locks. All that other stuff is O.K., but he's got to have power door locks.

We may think that's the dumbest thing we ever heard, but this is not the best time to share that opinion with the caller. *Support him.* Agree with him. Compliment his Dad's discretion and good judgment. Tell him how power door locks will contribute to his comfort, safety, and security. Don't discuss any of the other features, but restrict the conversation to his area of interest. The buyer will love you for it.

3. "CAN WE GET TOGETHER NOW, OR IS —————— BETTER?"

Go for it. You've invested money to get the call; don't lose the appointment by default. Go for it. The worst they can say is "no," and 20 percent of them will. That's why you need lots more questions to ask—to keep them on the phone.

A request for an appointment should not only be number 3, but number 6, 9, 12, 15, 18, 21, 24, 27, 30 . . . until the person says "yes" or hangs up.

Now, please take a few minutes and make a list of questions to put by your phone. Don't worry about words or grammar. As we've discussed, exact words are relatively unimportant and neatness doesn't count.

4. _____

5. _____

6. _____

7. _____

8. _____

9. _____

10. _____

11. _____

12. _____

13. _____

14. _____

15. _____

16. _____

17. _____

18. _____

19. _____

20. _____

5
REACH OUT AND PUT THE TOUCH ON SOMEONE

I've met a few people in my time who are enthusiastic about hard work. It was just my luck that all of them happened to be men I was working for at the time."

—*Bill Gold*

Everybody wants to buy your product. That's right, *everybody!* Some folks (motivated) want to buy it a lot. Other folks (nonmotivated) don't care whether they have it or not.

In any market, there are a given number of motivated buyers for your product or service at any given time. Only the most motivated of prospects (and therefore the best) will come to you. There are a far greater number of people who might well buy, if asked, but have not yet been sufficiently motivated to come in or call.

If we were to graphically depict the population of the world contained in a chemist's flask, heated by the flame of motivation, it might look like this.

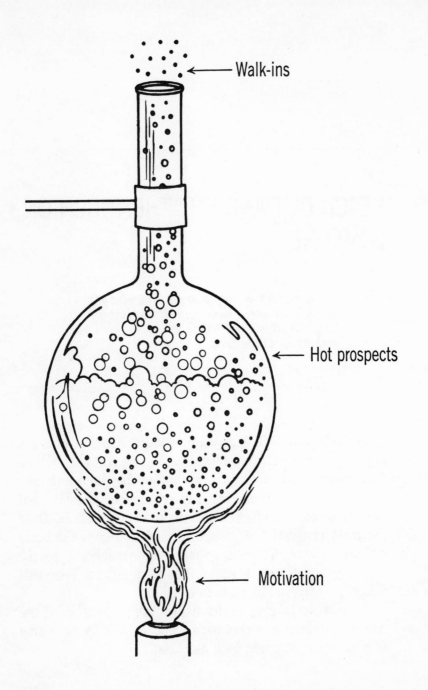

Walk-ins

Hot prospects

Motivation

We see that only the most motivated prospects stroll through the front door, leaving many potentially motivated prospects out there in the world for us. Wouldn't our lives be simplified if we could concentrate our efforts on those folks who want to buy our product and ignore all those who don't? Unfortunately, it doesn't work that way. We don't know who is motivated to buy, and *They don't either*. People, and their motivations, change daily.

This morning, a fellow in Des Moines got up, showered, kissed his wife, and went to work. He found he was to be transferred to Pittsburgh. This morning he didn't want to sell his house. This evening he does.

This morning a woman in San Diego got up, showered, kissed her husband, and went to work. She had a career adjustment meeting and was given the rubber key. There is a fine computer programmer available today who was not available yesterday.

This morning, on the way to work, a guy in Charlotte wrapped his car into a ball of foil. He was perfectly happy with the car, but now he needs a new one.

People, their circumstances, and their motivations change from minute to minute. Only by some method of consistent cold prospecting can we surprise people before they surprise us.

A cold call is defined, for our purposes, as calling someone you've never met who may or may not want to buy your product. One reason to make cold calls is to increase our odds of meeting qualified prospects. If this is our only reason, we're very likely to get depressed in short order. My records on cold calling reflect a ratio of appointments to calls of about 3 percent to 7 percent. That's a lot of "no's" for every "yes."

Robert Ringer, in his book *Looking Out for Number One*, sets forth the concept of:

"the retention of a positive mental attitude through the assumption of a negative result"

Positive thinkers tell us to approach each call with the firm belief that the call will result in a sale. *Bull.* The reality of the matter is that most people you call will *not* buy from you. If you call believing they will and they don't, depression will certainly ensue.

If, on the other hand, you call with the clear certainty that most people will say "no," your expectations are in tune with reality and you can keep at it. Occasionally, someone will say "yes" and your elation will know no bounds. It's much better for our mental health to assume the worst and take what comes, than to expect the best and live with perpetual disillusionment.

WHY MAKE COLD CALLS?

Why in the world, if we can't expect a high ratio of results, should we even bother with cold calling? A reasonable question, to which there are two answers.

1. To Make Money

I did not say that cold calling is unprofitable. I said that the measurable results are relatively low-yield. There is an immutable law with which all experienced salespersons are intimately familiar:

"You don't ask, you don't get"

I don't know how this law works, as I was not in on the original drafting of it; I only know it *does work*. If you prospect consistently and steadily, your business will be good. Many of your customers will come from sources not directly related to your prospecting efforts, but they will come. When you stop prospecting, the customers stop coming. That simple.

Now this is not to say that when you begin prospecting, you'll become instantly rich and famous. Doesn't work that way. It's rather like a hot water faucet—you've got to let it run a while before the water heats up. I don't know how that works either.

2. For Practice

Cold calls are the single greatest area of practice for salespeople. You can't possibly lose on a cold call because you didn't have anything going in. It's tough to practice on real, live, warm, motivated customers.

Since you don't know who you're calling, you can't possibly know what they're going to say. This keeps you sharp and mentally alert. Once you're into the swing of it, cold calls are actually *fun*.

WHY PEOPLE *DON'T* MAKE COLD CALLS

Now that we've discussed two reasons why making cold calls is a good idea, let's examine why we *don't* make cold calls and what we can do about it.

We Try to Make Too Many

At the first telephone sales seminar I attended, the instructor said that the only way to get results from cold calling was to "make 50 calls a day until you *die*." For me, death took about two days. Did you ever try to make 50 calls a *day?* It's like trying to eat an elephant. Now I don't care how much you love broiled elephant, it's tough to sit down and polish one off at one sitting. If we could keep the big devil fresh and just have a sandwich a day, though, given enough time we'd get him eaten.

One cold call an hour is plenty. Look at the numbers. If you make only one call an hour, eight hours a day, five days a week, that's 40 calls a week. At the end of a month you will have made 160 more calls than you are presently making. Do you honestly think 160 *extra* monthly calls wouldn't improve both your business and your telephone skills?

To aid in the discipline necessary to make the calls, I offer you a game. Any task we can have fun with is more easily done. The game is called "Test Your Guts."

First, get another salesperson as a partner. Then each hour, when Mickey's big hand hits twelve, you make a cold call and your partner gets to listen on the extension. Then he or she gets to make one while *you* listen on the extension. You'll tend to press each other to make the calls and critique the results. A great learning experience and fun in the bargain, as you discuss the peculiarities exhibited by the person you called.

If this doesn't yet sound like enough fun, try this. Each partner puts up a dollar bill, on which he has written "You beat me, you bastard" and signed it. The first person to get an appointment gets both the dollars and a symbol of the defeat of another human being. A barrel of laughs for more competitive types.

We Don't Know What to Say

Well, fortunately for you, *I* know what to say. I went to a seminar. I've been going to sales seminars all my adult life. That's how I got so misinformed.

The seminar leaders said you have to have a script. The

customers all have a script to get rid of you, so you have to have a script too. Seems only fair. The script should use the customer's name a lot, because that's supposed to flatter him and somehow short-circuits his brain. *Bull*.

I wrote a script and taped it by my phone where it would get all sweaty and yellow. It read like this:

ME: "Hello, Mrs. Schwartz?"

SHE: "Yes."

ME: "Thank you, Mrs. Schwartz. Mrs. Schwartz, [see, I used her name three times already] this is Hank Trisler calling from Waltz Realty. Am I taking you away from anything important?"

SHE: "Yes, you pervert." (Click, Buzzzzz)

I tried this approach for nearly six months before deciding it wasn't working too well. It suddenly occurred to me that I only wanted to know two things:

1. Do I have a decision-maker, the man or woman of the house? If I've got granny or the babysitter, I don't want to talk to them.
2. Do they want to buy what I'm selling? All else is unimportant. I've heard people talk about making calls for referrals, but the referrals I've gotten on cold calls aren't usually worth following up. I have no interest in bum referrals. I just want to know if *this person* is a potential buyer.

In line with these objectives, I developed this general approach:

ME: "Hi, Mrs. Schwartz?"

SHE: "Yes." [Good, one objective down. I've got the owner.]

ME: "Have you sold your home yet?"

This is a really terrific question, as it puts surprise on our side. Remember that in the last chapter, the customer called and scared us? Well, now it's our turn. The question is so blunt and sudden that the truth of the matter just pops out of the prospect.

> SHE: "I have no intention of selling my house, you pervert."

We have now fulfilled our call objectives. We reached the homeowner and she doesn't want to sell. The next phrase is very critical and should be repeated verbatim.

> ME: "Goodbye."

You may have noticed I didn't give my name. If she didn't want to sell, why is that important? If she wants to jump on somebody, I don't want it to be me. I only want her to know me if she's a potential buyer. It is far easier to dial another number than to deal with cantankerous people. Let's try another.

> ME: "Hello, Mr. Coors?"
> HE: "Yes."
> ME: "Have you bought your new word processor yet?"
> HE: "Yes. We just took delivery on a Phrase-O-Matic."
> ME: "Thank you. Good bye."

See how quickly these go? If you're trying for records in endurance, you can make 30 of these per hour. Let's dial again.

ME: "Hello, Mr. Shorthaul?"
HE: "Yes."
ME: "Have you bought your new truck yet?"
HE: "How did you know I wanted a new truck? Did my wife call you?"

Bingo!
Here's the beauty of this method of calling. The truth pops out and is almost always phrased differently. You can't get ready, as you don't know what they'll say, and *That keeps you sharp.*

"How could you know we wanted to sell? We only found out about the transfer this morning."
"I've been looking at word processors, but can't justify the price."
"Who told you I wrecked my truck?"

It's simply wonderful practice to respond to the unknown. If we all did this 160 times a month, would we be as likely to be thrown by the unexpected as we are now?

If you don't have the right answer on the tip of your tongue, don't worry. It'll come to you as soon as you're off the phone. It always does. There are always three sales presentations: (1) The one you were going to give, (2) the one you gave, and (3) the one you give yourself in the car on the way home. As soon as you're off the phone, the answer will come to you and you'll file it in your mind for future reference.

"Who told you to call me?" used to throw me into a tizzie. I always believe in being completely honest, but somehow "Well, I was cold popping in the phone book and just hit on you" seemed to lack a certain élan. For times like these, a friend of mine and I developed a method called "Creative Truth."

My friend, Cliff Brown, worked for the Connecticut General Life Insurance Company. We met for breakfast monthly with a brainstorming group, to exchange ideas and leads. As we'd part company each month, I'd say: "Cliff, your assignment this month is to contact 100 people with whom you have never spoken and inquire as to their needs for estate planning, or an insurance update." He'd say: "Great. And your assignment, Hank, is to contact 100 people you have never met and find out whether they want to buy or sell real estate." I'd agree and we'd shake on it to seal the bargain. Then when someone would say: "Who told you to call me?", I'd say: "Cliff Brown." And it was true.

You too will develop your unique methods of handling problems, but be prepared for the fact that the right phrase will not always pop readily to mind. Sometimes you're going to get stuck. Sometimes nothing works. Sometimes the most intelligent thing you can say is "errr——uhhh." When you find yourself mired in a mental cul-de-sac, *hang up.* That's right, hang up. If you stay on the phone when you're in trouble, two things will happen, neither one of them good.

1. You will only make matters worse. By continuing to run your mouth when brain function has ceased, you'll dig yourself in deeper, to the point of completely destroying any chances of a future relationship.
2. You'll scare the hell out of yourself. Mental meltdown is a frightening process to witness, much less endure. The longer you stay on the phone and squirm, the less likely you'll be to pick up the phone the next time. Be good to yourself: hang up. As soon as you're

off the hook, you'll think of thirty-two things you *should* have said.

Oh, I know what you're thinking. "If I go around hanging up on people, they'll hate me. They'll call me the hanging salesperson. I can't do that."

Yes you can. The only time hanging up is considered poor form is when the hangupee knows you have hung up. The key to having them not know you have hung up is: *Hang up while you're talking.*

No one in his right mind would hang up on himself, so they'll know you couldn't have done it. As soon as you've hung up, the panic will subside, you'll giggle a bit, and you'll think of all the things you could have said. Then, if you so desire, you can call back and say: "As I was saying when we were so rudely interrupted. . . ."

Learning to creatively hang up can put the fun back into cold calling.

Fear of Rejection

Salespeople all over the English-speaking world tell me the single biggest reason for not making cold calls is fear of how the callee will treat them. None of us really enjoys being treated badly.

Students of the behavioral sciences have been telling us for years that rejection is a chosen response. No one can reject you, they only reject your proposition. Rejection of you, as a person, is a response you choose for yourself.

I'm sure we can all understand, at the intellectual level, this premise. The problem is, rejection doesn't hurt you at the intellectual level, it hurts in the guts. Therefore, what we need is a method of dealing with rejection that appeals not to the intellect but to the viscera. Such a method is "paradoxical therapy."

Put simply, paradoxical therapy says: "Find that which you fear most and get yourself a truckload of it." You'll find the fear of the occurrence far exceeds the pain of the occurrence itself. If you fear heights, take up skydiving. How does this relate to selling? Paradoxical therapy can, in only one day, cure you of fear of rejection forever.

I first learned of this method in Seattle in the early 1960s. Seattle's major employer, Boeing Aircraft, had just lost the Dynasoar contract, and employment fell from 103,000 to 38,000 people in less than a month. At my company, business was so bad that even the people who didn't intend to pay weren't buying. We were selling funeral insurance (a fun business) for the Green Lawn Life Insurance Company of Boulder, Colorado, one of the industry biggies. It was hard to tell who had the worse attitude, the customers or the salespeople. We considered putting revolving doors on the front of the office to facilitate salesperson turnover. They simply couldn't handle the rejection.

Bob Quinn, our General Agent, struck upon the idea of paradoxical therapy. He could neither spell nor pronounce paradoxical therapy, so he just called it "Getting the crud kicked out of you."

Quinn had each of the salespeople pick 100 people at random from the phone book, call them, give his or her real name (we wanted to be sure the customers knew who they were going to reject), and offer to sell them one of three commodities: china, encyclopedias, or vacuum cleaners.

Why these products? For one thing, because nobody wants to buy them. Why else? We didn't have any to sell. Even if they said "yes," we couldn't win. The whole idea was to make 100 calls with the dead certainty of rejection on each one.

I chose vacuum cleaners and developed a canned pitch; I'll never forget it:

> ME: "Hello, Mrs. Gotrocks?"
> SHE: "Yes."
> ME: "Mrs. Gotrocks, my name is Hank Trisler from the Green Lawn Vacuum Cleaner Company. We have a terrific vacuum cleaner. Sits on four wheels, got a water pot on the bottom and little chrome cap on it—it'll suck all the dirt outa your rugs real good. Can I bring one out and show it to you?"
> SHE: "You @#$%¶&&*())+@#$%¶&*&*()+!"
> (Click, Buzzzzzz.)

Anything that doesn't kill you outright builds character, and this is a real character builder.

We have been doing this for years with our new salespeople, and it indeed is a fascinating process to observe. Am I going to tell you with a straight face that all our new salespeople made 100 of these calls? No way. Many people couldn't make it through the first half dozen, and left. Good. They undoubtedly saved themselves a lot of pain that they were going to experience if they went into selling. A healthy view of rejection is essential in this business.

The first half-dozen calls are the hardest. With each group we trained, the salespeople sweated profusely and sometimes shook so much that their finger slipped out of the dial hole and they got a wrong number. Actually, it doesn't matter who rejects you. We told them to talk to whoever answered.

After the first six calls, the beginning of therapy occurred. The salespeople began to talk to one another about the calls. Therapy is, after all, the ability of one person to express to another person what is going on in his world. They'd say: "You should have heard the one I just got. Never have heard such a mouth on a woman. She must drive a gravel truck. You should have heard what she said about Mom." The salespeople would discuss it and grin a bit, and the next call was just a little less frightening.

After about fifteen calls, a really amazing phenomenon occurred. The salespeople stopped talking to each other and started talking to the customers. "Please don't yell at me. I'm just trying to sell you china. There's no need to swear. My mother wasn't that way at all."

The realization was dawning, not intellectually but viscerally, that no matter how mad the customer got, he couldn't get his hands on you. His anger was his problem, unless we chose to make it ours.

After about 50 calls, the real confidence occurred. "Hey, a dirty talker. I had no idea when I called you that you wanted to talk dirty. Here's some words you haven't used yet: @#$¶%&*(+@%%$#*&*! Have a crappy day, you old bat!"

No one can reject you. Rejection is a chosen response. No one can embarrass you either. I didn't believe that, as all my life people had been telling me: "Don't do that, you embarrass me." Quinn proved me wrong again.

He had the first telephone amplifier I'd ever seen. It sat right up on his desk in two little boxes. Quinn didn't have a Cadillac, so the amplifier was his status symbol. He drove it everywhere. All his calls, incoming and outgoing, were amplified for all to hear.

His other status symbol was his office. He had a *big* office, which was good because it was the only office we had. One day we were having a sales meeting in his office, twenty-three salesmen sitting around his huge T-shaped desk. Green

Lawn's president and general sales manager were out from Boulder to get us all pumped up to sell lots of funeral insurance. It was a terrific meeting.

The phone rang and Bob answered it, which was good because he was great on the phone. Also good because we had no secretary.

> BOB: *"Good morning,* this is Green Lawn Life."
> VOICE: "I'd like to speak to Mr. Quinn, please."
> BOB: "You got him bunkie. What do you need?"
> VOICE: "Well sir, I'm the assistant manager at the Tradewell store out by your home. We have one of your checks here, it's been returned by the bank."

Now any normal mortal would have been decimated by this. I mean, the president of Green Lawn was there. I was so embarrassed for Bob that I wanted to crawl over his desk and yank the phone out of the wall, to somehow save him. Quinn didn't blush, he didn't even raise an eyebrow.

> BOB: "What the hell did they do that for?"
> VOICE: (Taken slightly aback) "Well, sir, the check was marked N.S.F."
> BOB: "Right. Now, as long as you're on the line, suppose you explain to me what N.S.F. means."
> VOICE: (increasingly rattled) "Well, sir, it means non-sufficient funds."
> BOB: "Oh bull. Have 'em run it through another bank. They can't all be out of money."

And he hung up.
No one can reject you.
No one can embarrass you.

6
WHERE THE RUBBER MEETS THE ROAD

"Success comes to those who know it isn't coming to them and go out and get it."

—Frank Tyger

You may be reading this book looking for the secret of success. Well, I don't know it. In observing thousands of successful salespeople over the past twenty-five years, I've found success methods to be as varied as the individuals themselves. Something that works well for me may be total anathema to you. Take door knocking. *Please.* I've never liked knocking on a strange door asking people to buy something, and therefore have never been really good at it. I do know a number of salespeople who have built a fine career based on their ability to knock on strange doors and convince people, completely unknown to them, to buy their product. I admire and respect these folks, but to get their methods, you'll have to buy their books.

In today's world, time and fuel costs mitigate against cold canvassing over a broad area. I much prefer to use the phone for cold prospecting and reserve my belly-to-belly time for people who at least have some interest in my services.

No, I don't know the secret of success, but I do know something of nearly equal value. I know the secret of failure. Why is this important? If you know the secret of failure, you can avoid it. Avoid failure and you should be getting closer to success. The secret of failure is:

TRY TO PLEASE EVERYBODY

When you try to please everybody, you end up pleasing nobody. Most important of all, you end up not pleasing *you*, and selling stops being fun. Your uniqueness is the greatest asset you have in selling. Trying constantly to conform to everyone else's opinion of what you *should* be diminishes that uniqueness, and is to be avoided at all cost.

Now here's the problem with being yourself. Someone might not like that. Be aware that every time you come into contact with a new prospect, he is going to make judgments about you. He is going to compare you to other people he's known and classify you as inferior or superior. We may not like that. We may not feel it is fair or nice, but that's the way people are. They're going to classify you, and we can't change that. Turnabout is, however, fair play. I believe that one of the more important lessons to be learned in selling is:

CLASSIFY YOUR CUSTOMERS

After having been at Seattle's First Repo Depo for an appropriate apprenticeship, I was contacted by Glen Green, the owner of Evergreen Chevrolet in Seattle. He asked me to become his Fleet and Truck Manager. I thought that odd, as I knew nothing of trucks. In fact, the only way I could tell a half-ton truck from a three-quarter-ton truck was, if they were side by side on the lot, the three-quarter-ton was about three inches taller.

My knowledge was not terribly important to Glen, as he knew nothing about trucks either. There were some 31 Chevrolet dealerships in the Seattle area, and in terms of truck sales, Glen was number 30. The only guy selling fewer Chevrolets than Glen was his brother John, out in Puyallup.

Then Glen said the magic words. He said, "I'll pay you $700 a month." I said, "Have your way with me."

He gave me a small office and a set of truck books. Did you ever try to read truck books? They are written in tongues. If you are born possessing the knowledge that G.V.W. means Gross Vehicle Weight and that G.C.W. means Gross Carrying Weight, reading the books is a snap. I was not so endowed and felt the books might as well have been written in Cantonese. I said, "Glen, I don't think I can be your truck manager. I can't read the damn books."

He said, "No sweat. We'll send you to a seminar. We'll send you to the G.M. Tech Center in Beaverton, Oregon, and for 2½ days you'll associate with the top truck pros in Washington, Oregon, Idaho, and Montana. At the end of those 2½ days you'll know more about trucks than you need to know."

I said: "*Oh, good!*" And I did indeed go to the G.M. Tech Center in Beaverton. And I did indeed associate with the top truck pros in Washington, Oregon, Idaho, and Montana. And I returned with two vital pieces of information that have served me well throughout my selling life. They were:

1. When ordering up a truck out of the truck books, don't never order nothing you don't understand. That

way you won't be surprised when the truck comes.

2. Order all your three-quarter-ton trucks red, so you can tell 'em from the half-tons on the lot.

Armed with this essential knowledge, I tucked my books under my arm and went out to call on the owners of businesses. The seminar had said that, when making a cold call, you ought to have a snappy opening. I developed one. I'd say: "Hi, I'm Hank Trisler from Evergreen Chevrolet. You don't want to buy a truck, do you?" They'd say, "No," and I'd leave.

After a couple of months, Glen said maybe I needed something a shade more positive. So I learned how to say: "Hi. I'm Hank Trisler from Evergreen Chevrolet. You bought your new truck yet?" Isn't that better?

They'd say, "No," and I'd go away.

One afternoon I was down south of Seattle in the little town of Renton. I went into a lumberyard owned by a creative fellow named Ralph. He called the place Ralph's Lumber. Standing in the yard was a tall, spare man in bib overalls and a big hat. I said: "You Ralph?"

He said: "Yep."

I said: "Hi. I'm Hank Trisler from Evergreen Chevrolet. You bought your new truck yet?"

He said: "No, but I'm sure glad you came by. I need a lumber truck."

I thought: "Oh Christ."

You see, my problem was that I had already told him more than I knew about trucks. I got my books out of my pickup, went into his office, and helped him with the only decision on which I was qualified to advise. We decided to order him a green one.

Now I don't suppose you've ever ordered up a truck from Chevrolet, so I'll tell you how it works. You don't just call

Chevrolet and order a lumber truck. All Chevrolet sells you is a cab and chassis. The cab is the part where the man sits, with the windows and seats and steering wheel. The chassis is nothing to brag about at all. Just two black iron rails sticking out of the back of the cab. It has big wheels on the back, which is good, otherwise those rails would just drag on the ground. That's all Chevrolet sends you, and it takes them six weeks at that. The rest you have to buy locally.

I went down to the Utility Body Company and said: "Hi, I'm Hank Trisler from Evergreen Chevrolet. I want a flat bed body for a $2^1/_2$-ton lumber truck."

He said: "Wonderful. Give me your specs."

I thought: "I don't know what he wants with my glasses, but if it'll help me get that flat bed body, he can have 'em."

He was an obliging sort of fellow, so he helped me design the body for Ralph's truck. I didn't go to Detroit and watch them build the truck, but I went daily to the Utility Body Company to oversee the construction of that flat bed body.

It was beautiful. It had white douglas fir planks and black iron strapping all around the outside. Stake pockets. Big black rubber mud flaps with white raised letters spelling "Utility." Huge red reflectors and amber running lights. I formed an unnatural emotional attachment.

The day I had been breathlessly awaiting finally arrived. Ralph's truck came in. I took it to the sign shop and had "Ralph's Lumber" emblazoned on both doors. I took it to the Utility Body Company and personally supervised the torquing of every bolt to be sure the body was secure. It was absolutely beautiful and I was *so* excited.

I borrowed a Polaroid camera and proudly took Ralph's new truck out for delivery. When I arrived, I said: "Ralph. I've got your new truck and it's simply beautiful. I wonder if you'd do me a personal favor. As you know, this is my first big truck sale, and I'm so excited about it. I wonder if you and your foreman would pose by the truck—don't stand in front of the signs—and I'll take your picture. In fact, I'll take two pictures and I'll keep the one that turns out better for my scrapbook, so I'll have a photo record and can remember this day *forever*."

Ralph, too, was an obliging kind of fellow. He said: "Absolutely, and just to make this picture more realistic, we'll throw a load of lumber on that truck."

I shouted: "*Oh good!!*"

That's the day I learned what "H.D. Springs" means. You see, in the truck book it didn't say "Heavy Duty Springs." It just said "H.D. Springs," and I didn't understand it, so I didn't order them because I didn't want to get surprised. When we put the lumber on the truck, it just sort of *squatted*. The lumber just eased down to rest on the top of the wheels. It still looked beautiful, but it was definitely squatting.

Ralph said: "Hank." And I just knew he was talking to *me*.

I said: "Yeah, Ralph?"

He said: "If you were to hazard a wild guess, what do you reckon that truck's doing?"

I said: "Well, now, Ralph, I'm not *real* sure, but it sort of looks like it's squatting. Ain't it just a beauty though?"

He said: "Yeah, it's pretty enough, but the way it is, it won't roll. I sorta had in mind buying a lumber truck that'd roll."

Then he began to laugh. He took off his big hat and hit me with it, laughing hysterically.

He gasped: "Ain't that just the gawddamndest looking truck you ever saw? The thing is *squatting!*"

He laughed so hard that he got me laughing, as bad as I felt. Here I know I'm going to have to spend my money on overload springs, and *I'm* laughing. I wish you could have been there to see it: three o'clock on a drizzling Thursday afternoon in a Renton lumberyard, two idiots whooping, slapping at each other, and dancing around a squatting lumber truck. Ralph laughed so hard, a tear rolled down his leg.

I learned something very valuable about people that day. There is a category of customers I call "A" customers, who love you even when you screw up. Anybody who does business the way I do business *needs* "A" customers. In fact, anybody at all needs "A" customers.

Besides their being great people, there's another beauty of "A" customers. Every person you know has a major influence on the buying decisions of at least five other people. If you have only 100 "A" customers who like you, trust you, believe you, and will send you business, you can become involved in the buying decisions of at least 500 people. For most of us, that would make for a pretty fair year. Now granted, TV advertising reaches millions of people, but you can't know, or be known by, millions of people. All you need is 100 "A's" or, as I sometimes think of them, "Spheres of influence."

Not only will spheres of influence make money for you, they'll make your selling life more enjoyable too. As we discussed earlier, we are drawn to people like ourselves. Here's the great part of that song. If you're my "A" customer and you send me buyers, the odds are great that they will be people like you and I will like them and they will like me, just as you do. *That's wonderful.* It means I get to spend time working with people who like me. A salesperson's dream.

If, on one end of a continuum, we have "A's," is it not reasonable to assume that on the other end of the continuum we'd have "C's"? Let me stress, "C's" are not people you don't like. I've sold to lots of people I don't like, and their money spends as well as anybody else's. "C's" are people who don't like you—and share that information with you. "C's" are people who make you feel inadequate by constantly pointing out how you fail to measure up to *their* perception of what you should be. "C's" make you feel bad about you, and therefore diminish your ability to function well in selling.

I'm not crazy about trying to put people in categories or pigeonholes, because each person is an individual. There are, however, some people with whom I simply cannot get along. This is not because I don't like them; it's because they don't like me. "C's" for me are accountants and schoolteachers. They want someone to be precise. Precision has never been my strong suit. A schoolteacher wants you to spell a word the same way *every time*. I figure if I've got most of the letters in the word, it's right. Mark Twain said: "Anyone who cannot spell any word at least two ways has no imagination." An accountant goes on a tennis court not to play tennis, but to see if the lines are straight. He'd marry Farrah Fawcett for her money. I drive these people nuts, and they me.

I decided to give all my "C's" to Fred Smith. There was a good reason for picking Fred. I didn't like him much. Now that makes sense. If I gave people who didn't like me to someone I liked, nobody would be any better off. Fred was patient, empathetic, gentle, obtuse, diplomatic, and more than a little dull. He was everything I was not, and my "C's" loved him. They would sit together and fiddle with numbers for *hours* and leave happy. Everybody won. Fred got a deal, I got a piece of it, the company made a sale, and the customers got what they wanted. So I determined to give all my "C's" to Fred Smith—except for aerospace engineers.

At that time, in Seattle, we had a breed of cat, aerospace engineers, who dressed much as they must have when they were in the seventh grade. Brown shoes with crepe soles, and white socks. Tweed jackets with leather patches on the sleeves. White sidewall haircuts. They had a way of getting 17 pens in their breast pocket, along with a slide rule. They smoked big, black, droopy pipes. Each of them looked like a Bessemer blast furnace blowing slag over his shoulders when he walked. They were hyperprecise, dominant, hostile, and surly. They commenced all conversations with: *"I want. . . ."* These guys would *destroy* me. I knew that if I talked to one of them for more than twenty continuous seconds, it would take me two weeks at home in bed, electric blanket turned up to nine, living on nothing but graham crackers and warm milk, before I could even *shave.* Aerospace engineers I gave to Turk McGuire.

Turk was a great guy. He was 6'4½" tall, had a waxed handlebar mustache, and shaved his head. He used to be a sergeant with the Denver police force, but was discharged for unnecessary roughness. Sometimes, when he walked, he stepped on his fingers. I'd see an aerospace engineer striding purposefully across the street, smoke billowing over his shoulder, and I'd run to the back room, where we kept Turk, and get him.

The engineer: "I want. . . ."

Turk: "Don't you tell *me* what you want. You follow me and I'll show you what we've got." *And they would!*

It was wonderful. If I talked to them that way, they'd kill me, but Turk McGuire, they followed. That was good, because if *he* didn't get *them, they* were going to get *me.*

We salespeople are too valuable and emotional to spend a lot of time with people who make us nervous or worse. True, if we are perpetually in contact with people we find unpleasant, we can probably make them more pleasant. That's the way it is, we sort of rub off on one another. But this means that they, in return, will usually make us less pleasant and harm our self-image. If you have "C" people in your life, *get rid of them.* They will destroy you. None of us are going to get out of this world alive. The number of people who attend your funeral will largely be determined by the weather on that day. If you go on a good June day, you'll draw a big crowd; but if you go in February, you're going to do it alone. Between now and then, doesn't it just make good sense to take care of the only person who's *sure* to show up? The secret of failure is trying to please everybody.

A "B" customer is one who neither falls in love with you in the parking lot, nor hates you on sight. "B's" are the great majority of our customers. I view my job, as a sales professional, as turning a "B" into an "A" as soon as possible. Failing that, I'll try to sell him without major damage to either of us. Failing that, I'll classify him as a "C" and give him away before he really hates me. Selling's a simple business.

Let's run through the three classifications of customers again and how each should be handled.

"A" customers will send you business.

I believe that the easiest, fastest, most pleasant, and most profitable method of prospecting is getting referrals from our spheres of influence—spheres usually created by

"A's." Love your "A's." Take an "A" to breakfast or lunch every week. Write them notes. Remember them on special holidays, their birthdays, and the anniversary of their purchase. An "A" will send you business, if he remembers you. So never forget an "A," and never let an "A" forget you.

"B" customers will give a referral, if asked.

In asking for referrals, with either "A" or "B" customers, two things are very important to remember:

1. *Ask early.* The customer will seldom be more enthusiastic about his purchase than he is on the day it arrives. As soon as the delivery of the product or service is completed, we must ask for referrals. "Tell me, who else do you know who might enjoy owning a —————?" Notice the nondirective probe using "who." This question cannot be answered "yes" or "no" and is more likely to result in a name.

2. *Ask often.* Every time you contact a "B," ask for business. A "B" may remember you personally, but forget what you sell. Spaced repetition is one of the finest ways to learn. Spaced repetition is a method of learning whereby one is repeatedly exposed to material over an extended time frame. Complete the following sentences: A stitch in time saves —————. People who live in glass houses shouldn't throw —————. Our customers learn the same way, and they'll learn to send us business if we merely ask for business repeatedly.

Some people are boggled by the broad question: "Who do you know who needs to buy a —————?" Let's help our customers in their thought processes by breaking the population of the world down into more manageable groups.

"Who do you know at work who needs a new car?"
"Who do you know in your neighborhood who might
be moving?"

> "Who else, in your field, might need relief from poor paper flow?"

By dealing with smaller groups, our customers can focus on individuals and may well find a suspect for us.

The bottom line is to keep asking. Our customers will learn to associate our name with our product or service. When they think of *doogers*, they'll think of us. They'll also learn that when they see us, they will be gently asked for business. The unconscious reaction is to get business for us so they'll pass the test. No one likes to flunk tests.

"C" customers will not send you business.

Neutralize these customers so they will not bad-mouth you when asked for an opinion. Let's try our level best to be civil and even helpful to these folks, so that when they are asked about our competence, integrity, and personal hygiene, they'll not speak unkindly of us.

Now we have a referral, so all we have to do is go out and sell them our doogers, right? Have a good positive attitude, tell them our story, and they'll buy, right? *Bull.* Do you sell every qualified lead you get? Of course not. No one does. We all blow leads, even referrals. That's just the way selling goes. Selling has been described as a process of throwing a lot of stuff up against the wall. Some sticks, some falls off. One thing is absolutely certain, however: if we don't throw any up, none will stick. The only people who don't blow deals are the ones who don't try to put any together. The more productive we are, the more failure we'll experience.

Most professional salespeople understand this. I'm always puzzled, therefore, when speaking with salespeople in various parts of the world, that the phrase "My deal is blowing up" is often preceded by *"Oh my God. . . ."* From their tone of voice and the panic in their eyes, you'd think it was the last sale they'd ever have. Whenever you're blowing a sale, or a referral, be comforted by this fact: according to recent census, there are now 960 million Chinese. They didn't even know you *had* a deal.

The important thing is not whether you blew the referral, but how you *and the referring source* feel about the failure. Let's face it, if the person who gave you the referral feels badly about the failure, your referral source will have dried up. That's far more critical than any lost sale.

The key to maintaining a favorable relationship with the person who gave you the referral is *speed*. Whenever a referral is blown, a race ensues. The person who first conveys the news of the blown deal to the referring source, wins.

To clarify, let's look at an example. I am referred by my friend, Gordon Goodguy (an "A" if there ever was one) to Randolph Ratfink, a prospect for our new Super Dooger. I try my very best to sell our Super Dooger, but Randolph buys a Dooger from Dilbert's Doogers, conclusively proving he has no taste whatever.

Two days later, at lunch with Gordon, Randolph says: "Well, I bought my new dooger."

Gordon: "Great. I knew old Hank would take good care of you."

Randolph: "I didn't buy from Hank. I bought a Dilbert's Dooger. Their price was better and I got the color I wanted."

Gordon Goodguy has been discounted. He gave me an obviously qualified and motivated lead, and I blew it. Randolph could have bought our dooger, but bought Dilbert's instead. Gordon not only is miffed at having his referral discounted by Randolph; he begins to doubt his own wisdom in buying our Super Dooger. Does Randolph know something that he doesn't?

Let's contrast this to the situation where I get to Gordon before Randolph does. *The instant* I find the deal is dead, I call Gordon and say: "Thank you very much for referring me to Randolph Ratfink. He bought a new dooger and he's delighted with it."

Gordon: "Great. I knew you'd take good care of him."

Me: "I really tried to, but he bought a Dilbert's Dooger instead."

Gordon: "What?"

Me: "Yes. He apparently wasn't as interested in quality as you are. Initial price was his primary consideration, so Dilbert's was the obvious choice. That really isn't important, though. What's really important is that he's happy, and that's all either of us wanted, isn't it?"

Is not Gordon's reaction likely to be totally different? Here he has exposed Randolph to the finest dooger available, sold by the finest salesperson, and Randolph didn't have the God-given good sense to recognize the opportunity. Gordon will redouble his efforts to get us a customer with better taste. The only difference in forming his attitude is who got there with the bad news first. To repeat, when a referral is blown, the person who gets to the referring source first wins.

Our reaction on those happy times when we *don't* blow the deal is even more important. The likelihood of our receiving a continuing stream of referral business will be determined by our treatment of our referring source when we succeed. Let's call him immediately to tell him how happy both we and the customer are. This will vindicate his judgment in sending us the referral in the first place.

When one of our "A's" or "B's" sends us business, it is

an act of love. We must give lots of love in return. All "A's" should be sent cards and notes and taken out to a meal from time to time. With special "A's," buy them presents. Not the standard kind of "volume builders" that specialty sales-people sell, with your company advertising printed all over them. Choose real presents, selected just for them. A sweater. A pair of slacks. A painting. A special putter. Something that reflects thought and caring. The cost of the gift is unimportant. Some gifts costing the least will have the greatest impact, if they clearly were chosen with care.

Some of your referring sources will be in positions where the receipt of gifts would be inappropriate or embarrassing. But I know of no policy anywhere to preclude one from having dinner with a friend. Take these customers to lunch or dinner, and share with them your greatest gift: *you.*

I have gotten best results by never mentioning that the gift or meal is, in any way, tied to the receipt of a referral. It's not a reward for good behavior; that's the way we train dogs. I present the gift merely as evidence of my esteem and friendship for the person.

Never give money. The principal difference between prostitutes and lovers is money. I don't care whether it's ethical or legal in your field, don't do it. If the value of the relationship is based on money, someone else can always come along and outbid you. Don't make hookers out of your friends.

Treat your "A's" and "B's" as you would like to be treated. Love them, help them, and *ask them for business.*

If you've been selling your line for over two years and are not doing over 80 percent repeat and referral business, you're working too hard. For years they've been telling me: "When the going gets tough, the tough get going." *Bull.* That does not align with my perception of reality. When the going gets tough, the truly professional salesperson looks around to see what the hell's wrong. Masochism is not the hallmark of the professional.

Work with referrals for easier and more profitable selling.

7
WHY DON'T YOU EVER WRITE ME?

*"The difference between intelligence and
education is this: intelligence will make you a
good living."*

—*Charles F. Kettering*

Oh, I know you *hate* to write. So do I. Yes, I understand
your handwriting is illegible, your grammar abominable,
and your punctuation nonexistent. I too am guilty of all of
the above, a fact to which the editor of this book will readily
attest.

Neil Green, a friend of mine in Sydney, Australia, tells
beautifully the story of the "begging letter." It seems that
Australia has a national lottery, wherein one can win as
much as a million dollars. Upon publication of the winner's
name, said winner is promptly inundated with "begging
letters," asking for money for treatment of illnesses, someone's college education, a new car, or any other of a myriad
of seemingly plausible causes. When one hits the honey

barrel, hundreds, indeed thousands, of folks write "begging letters" to try to get a piece of the action.

A gentleman, upon reading the morning paper, was ecstatic to find he was the big winner and so informed his wife. She asked, "But dear, what about the begging letters?" He replied, "Keep on sending them."

This strikes me as an extremely fine bit of business advice. Here's the bottom line. Fuel costs, telephone costs, and the per hour value of your time are all on the increase. Writing to your customers is one of the easiest, least costly means of keeping in touch. Phrased another way, you will *make more money* by writing to people. Now do I have your attention? Well then, let's proceed.

I am sick and tired of corresponding with computers. My name is not "Occupant" or "Resident," so I'll throw away, unopened, any mail so addressed. I also have a great deal of difficulty relating to any correspondence addressed on stick-on labels or computer-printed.

I'm only slightly more enthusiastic about typewritten letters. Any typewritten letters I get are likely to be long and boring. They probably want me to give money for something, buy something, or do something for them for free. The worst letters of all, invariably typewritten, are from lawyers, asking me to answer hard questions. I hate hard questions.

Conversely, real letters or cards, handwritten by real people, with real stamps, personally licked, are eagerly anticipated but seldom received. I love to get handwritten letters, as they are usually short and interesting, say nice things, and seldom ask truly hard questions. When an envelope bearing an almost illegible scrawl appears on my desk, I go for it first. I rip it open feverishly and devour the contents. I know how hard writing is. If you think enough of me to write me a note, I sure as hell think enough of you to read it. I have to believe I'm not all that different, in this regard, from most folks. People *like* to receive hand-written notes. My job, as a sales professional, is to make people happy. If they want notes, then I'm sure going to write 'em notes.

There are some ideas on writing notes that have served me well.

KEEP THEM SHORT

Most of us neither like to read, nor write, long letters. They take up too much time. Until you get the hang of it, short letters are actually more difficult to write than long ones. They require thought. Someone once wrote, "I'd have written a shorter letter, but I didn't have time."

A good rule of thumb is to keep your notes to three sentences, maximum. Think about what you want to say, say it, and sign it.

At my organization, for all our note correspondence, we have abandoned standard letterhead sheets ($8^1/_2 \times 11$) and have gone to half-sheets ($5^1/_2 \times 8^1/_2$). These not only look more like personal notes, as opposed to business letters, but being smaller, they're easier to fill up. A good business note should be able to be written by a person, standing in a phone booth, in less than a minute.

I know it sounds hard, but practice will make it automatic.

HANDWRITE THEM

People open handwritten mail and tend to read every word. Don't worry about your penmanship. Neatness doesn't count.

They lied in school. What counts is that you cared enough to put pen to paper and write. You gave a little bit of yourself.

I have a very special friend, Warren Ringer, who lives a fair distance from me. He sends me poetry. He'll send me a little handwritten "Poem to Celebrate Spring" or a "Special Poem for Your Birthday" or a "Poem Because I Miss You." There are some problems with Warren's poems. He can't spell and can't rhyme. It doesn't matter to me. I don't like poetry anyhow, but I'd crawl over a mile of broken glass to read Warren's notes. He cares about me and shows it.

Another advantage of handwritten notes is that they're easier to keep short. Think about it. Most of us write bigger than a typewriter does. This means if we handwrite a note, it'll take fewer words to fill up a page. This helps us gain our objective of short letters, which take less time to write and read.

Toward this end, years ago I bought a fountain pen with a broad nib. It throws a wide line and pumps ink like a fire hose. With this, I write even bigger and can get far fewer words on the page. Only problem is, it uses so much ink that I spend all the time I save just filling the pen.

HAND STAMP THEM

Postage meters imply institutional mail, which is to be avoided. Stamps are messy, but again, they show you *care*.

CONSIDER THE THREE MAGIC PHRASES

There are three magic phrases in note-writing: *thank you*, *congratulations*, and *thinking of you*. Notes that start with one of these three phrases are read voraciously. They set the stage for a warm and friendly communication. Let's take each in turn.

"Thank You"

There is not a person living who hears this enough. We're all starved for "Thank you's," and they're easy to say.

"Thank you, Stan, for the pleasure of your company at lunch today. . . ."

"Thank you, Hortense, for taking time from your busy schedule to see me today. . . ."

"Thank you, Farley, for returning my call so promptly. . . ."

"Thank you, Felicia, for your order for 5,000 doogers. . . ."

"Thank you, Gordon, for your referral to Randolph Ratfink. . . ."

When we thank people for what they've done, we predispose them to do more of it. People need constant reinforcement. I read once, I know not where:

> Do you love me
> or love me not?
> You told me once,
> but I forgot.

"Congratulations"

A number of years ago, I bought 5,000 cards with "Congratulations" printed on the front and our company name on the back. They folded in half and were blank inside, to provide room for notes to be written by our salespeople. Like most tools management buys for salespeople, they were seldom used. I found them in desk drawers, in the trunks of cars, and used for telephone messages.

Rather than just waste them, I mailed out 500 blank ones to people I knew, predicated on the assumption that nearly everyone has done *something* within the past two weeks for which he feels he should have been congratulated. The response was amazing. People would call in and say: "Thanks for your card. How did you *know*??" This left me with yet another problem, but at least they called.

"Congratulations, Barnaby, on your decision to own. . . ."

"Congratulations, Jan, on your well-deserved promotion. . . ."

"Congratulations, Jose, on your new arrival. . . ."

"Congratulations, Diana, on your anniversary. . . ."

"Congratulations" is one of the sweetest words ever to fall upon your ears, particularly if you are a person of considerable accomplishment. You hear that word so seldom. The higher you climb, the fewer people there are around you to tell you that you are doing a good job. Remember when you were the new kid and brought in your first deal? Everyone was so excited. They said, "Attaboy," "You done *good*," and "You're gonna be *great*." Now you are in the top five in your company, and when you bring in a deal, the same people say "Lucky stiff" and "Look, Martha, another no-brainer." All people of accomplishment experience this. It goes with the territory. Vinegar Joe Stillwell said, "The higher you climb, the more your rear is exposed." Everyone you know needs to feel he is doing well and *someone else knows it*.

"Thinking of You"

We spend so much time worrying about what people think about us, when they so seldom do. Whenever someone lets me know he was actually thinking about me, I'm flattered to the point of digging my toe in the dirt.

"Thinking of you" is a good all-purpose salutation—something to say when you can't think of anything else to say. It's always true, too. You must have been thinking of them, or you couldn't have written.

"Thinking of you, Blair, and of how long it's been since we chatted. . . ."

"Thinking of you, Chris, and of how great you'd look in a new Belchfire 4. . . ."

"Thinking of you, Doris. You've owned your Super Dooger a year now and. . . ."

"Thinking of you, Bob, and how the new tax law will affect. . . ."

KEEP THEM GOING OUT

Slumps often result from the fact that when our business is booming and orders are rolling in, we tend to become lax in our prospecting efforts. When our business stinks, we prospect like crazy because we haven't anything else to do. This is contrary to the dictates of good, common horse sense. When business is bad, it is commonly held that people, by and large, don't want to buy. Intensified advertising and prospecting efforts only tend to put us in touch with ever increasing numbers of people who don't want to buy. This can bring about aggravated depression and a need to write all letters with crayons to avoid contact with sharp objects.

Conversely, when business is great, people want to buy and increased prospecting puts us in touch with more of those people, who will give us money and make us grin. "Make hay while the sun shines." It doesn't make sense to throw time and money after a bad market. It does make sense to keep a constant flow of "begging letters" going out, good market or bad. In a good market, they'll bring you even more prospects. In a bad market, they'll keep you in touch with all your customers, some of whom *may* want to buy, even in a bad market. Some of our customers are so sheltered and obtuse that they don't even know the market is bad and continue to do business anyhow.

Sending "begging letters" in a down market makes sense, especially as the coefficient of direct rejection is so low. The last thing a demoralized salesperson needs is more rejection. If you mail out 100 letters and no one calls you to buy, that's not good, but it isn't horrible either. If you make 100 phone calls and everyone hangs up on you, that's not good at all. If you knock on 100 doors and they all slam on your face, that's bad. When you go home and find your wife has moved, that's *real bad*. The more closely involved we are, the more intense and personal rejection becomes. If you're already feeling down and out, you don't need more rejection. Try "begging letters."

THE TIPS SYSTEM

After I had been in selling a few years, I found my referral business was not very strong. If someone came back to buy from me, it was by purest chance; I had no systematic method of contacting past buyers on a regular basis. In reviewing my customers' files, I found I had not talked to most of them since they bought. Oh, there were a few of them I saw regularly. Social contacts, friends, club members. But the vast majority of my customers had been abandoned. I determined that what I needed was a really good follow-up system. Immediately I embarked on a very nearly lifetime search for *the ultimate system*.

My first system was dy-no-mite. It involved two black binders with lots of snap rings and removable customer information sheets. One book had alphabetical indexes. The other had indexes for each month of the year and 1 to 31 indexes for each day of the month. If one of my prospects said he planned to buy after school was out, I'd move his card to June. When June came, I'd move the card to the appropriate day and call him then. The system was great, as it required a lot of time to manage and thereby minimized the amount of time I had to spend with customers, risking rejection.

Another key advantage to the system was that every day I had something to do. I'd sit down and call all the people whose cards said they might buy from me.

ME: "Hi. This is Hank. Have you bought your new truck yet?"

HE: "Yeah. We bought a *Ford*." I'd tear up the card.

ME: "Hi. This is Hank. I have a note here to call you today about your interest in a new truck."

HE: "Lost my job. Can't buy now. Call me in the fall." I'd move the card to September.

ME: "Hi. This is Hank. We talked about a new truck. You told me to call you today."

HE: "We overhauled the motor on the old one. Ought to last another year or so."

I'd move the card to next year.

Every morning I went through this drill. It consumed a good two to three hours and often made me feel so useful that I didn't need to prospect anymore at all that day.

One day, deep in the middle of a slump (I hadn't sold a truck in three weeks), I was busily following my plan when Bill Hamilton, the General Sales Manager, walked in. He said: "What the hell are you doing anyhow?"

I proudly showed him my system, replete with yellow, curled, sweat-soaked prospect sheets.

He said: "That's interesting. Let me see those a minute."

Beaming with the glow reserved for those who know they are doing the "right thing," I handed over my most precious possession for his inspection and approval. Giggling with unbridled glee, he took off like a scalded dog and threw my books in the incincerator. In a flash they were gone, along with any hope I had of ever becoming a master truck salesman.

I was undone. There was no reason for my continued existence. I went home, sat in front of the TV and sucked my thumb until it got all white and wrinkled. Two days later, Bill called:

> BILL: "Are you gonna pout forever, or are you coming back to work?"
> ME: "There's no reason to come back. I haven't got anybody to work on."
> BILL: "Well then, I guess you'll just have to go and get some fresh meat."

In the next two weeks, I sold six trucks. The experience convinced me that follow-up is necessary, but never to the exclusion of taking care of the business of the day.

Over the years I have owned, and attempted to operate, some of the most esoteric and arcane systems known to man. I bought a card system so heavy I couldn't lift it. Customers were filed by assigned number and cross-referenced to an alphabetical index, date of purchase, birth date, and wedding anniversary. It was so complex that I had to hire someone part-time to run it, as I didn't clearly understand it. It lasted about six months.

I subscribed to a computerized follow-up system. They sent hand-signed, commemorative stamped cards at specified intervals. My customers kept asking me why my signature on the cards was so different from that which appeared elsewhere. I dropped that system too.

I finally had to face reality. I needed a system which personally involved me and which was simple. If it's very complicated, I simply can't do it. Simplicity was the cornerstone. I researched the English language and came upon an amazing revelation. The English alphabet, in *every* state in the union and *all* the provinces of Canada, contains exactly 26 letters. No more, no less.

TIPS was born.

TIPS stands for Trisler's Idiot-Proof System, again based on the premise that if it's hard, I can't do it. Further extended, if I can do it, *anybody* can do it.

I got a metal card file box and filed everyone I knew alphabetically. That's right, *everyone*. Friends, sold customers, prospects, everyone. The first week, I contacted everyone whose last name started with A or B, the next week, everyone whose last name started with C or D, and so forth. Since there are 26 letters in the alphabet, this means I contact everyone I know every 13 weeks, or roughly four times a year. Every Monday I pull out the appropriate cards and make decisions. If they merit a call, I call them and follow with a "thank you" note. If they don't merit a call, I write them a "thinking of you" card.

This simplifies my life, and I like that. Do I sometimes lose some business because they want to buy during the 13-week interval between calls? Sure. But look at all the time I've saved by not following bad leads. Besides, if I've done my job right, they just may call me when they're ready.

The TIPS system is not only simple to operate, it's cheap too—an important consideration for the frugal among us. All you need is:

1 file box

1 alphabetical index

1 lot of file cards

1 paper clip

Paper clip? Oh yes, I forgot to mention that. You need a paper clip to move along the alphabetical index cards so you can remember which letters you're working on.

Using the TIPS system and writing "thank you" cards for all calls and contacts, I can achieve my daily goal of 10 cards mailed. Why not write a note *right now?*

8
WORKING SMART, NOT HARD

*"The time to relax is when you don't have time
for it."*

—*Sydney J. Harris*

Early in my selling career, I had a boss who loved to say:
"We only want you to work half a day here—and we don't
care which twelve hours it is. That's the way we do it here.
Sales meetings at 8:00 A.M. Five-dollar fine for any fool who
is late. Work, work, work. Make calls. Words alone will
often fail, you've got to *demonstrate* to make that sale.
Close early, close often, close hard. Keep your eye on the
ball, your nose to the grindstone, your shoulder to the wheel."
You ever try to get anything done in that position?

I long ago determined that I'm never going to exceed J.
Paul Getty in net worth. Besides, he's dead. I don't have
any interest in seeing how much money I can amass in my
estate. They don't put pockets in shrouds. I merely want
to make enough to buy really nice toys. Now what's the

sense in having really nice toys, if you have no time to play with them?

I'm further going to suggest to you that simply working hard doesn't get it in today's market. We have to be more creative than the other person, and it is flatly impossible to be creative when you're running full throttle. We get creative while lying on our backs, looking at the horsies and duckies in the clouds. A fellow named Guggenheim, who founded the interestingly named Guggenheim Steel & Smelting empire, was recently quoted in *Forbes*: "The person who works twelve months a year, does not really work twelve months a year. It is the person who works ten or eleven months and does something entirely different for one or two months, who *really* works twelve months a year."

Years ago, top salespeople told me they worked 70 to 80 hours a week and I believed them. I also worked 70 to 80 hours a week and found that I really didn't like selling all that much. Then I began to notice that the *truly* top salespeople were working 30 hours a week, maybe 40 under extreme duress, and making more money than I was. I tried that and it *worked*. The key here is to really work when you work. Then when you're done, get out of the store and relax, so you feel like working the next day.

Here's the problem. In sales it's very difficult to know when you're done. When business is strong, we work like fools to capitalize on a strong market. When business stinks, we work like fools to try to make it better. In short, it's tough to try to find a convenient time for recreation and relaxation. This dilemma usually arises from a lack of clear-cut goals and objectives.

"Oh no," you say, "He really isn't going to get on the old goal bandwagon, is he?" Yes, I am, but with a slightly different approach. Please bear with me.

Most goal-setting courses you and I have attended state that, to be effective, goals must be specific and clearly written, have a clear time frame, and, in general, be hard to do. That's why most people don't set them.

Goals *should* be specific. Our subconscious mind, which controls our behavior, only understands ideas that are specific. That needn't mean *hard* ideas, just clear ones. In fact, if you can't write a goal on the back of a business card, it probably isn't clear enough.

Goals *should* be written. Not necessarily to be read every day, but because writing goals down increases the likelihood of clarity. Goals that are simply visualized, or verbalized, tend to be hazy and ambiguous. Reducing them to writing makes them crisp and clear and readily assumable by the subconscious.

Goals *should not* have a time frame. Assume we say, "I will earn $50,000 this year." Two things might happen, neither one of them good:

1. According to a variation of Murphy's Law, "Any task will expand to completely consume the time allocated for its completion." This means if we hit a really big lick and earn $50,000 by August, we tend to shuffle paper for the rest of the year, so we end up with $50,000. This is not a conscious plan, but a subconscious reaction to keep our production consistent with our self-image.

2. A goal that has a specific time frame which is too long, tends to motivate us too late. A $50,000 annual goal becomes real and important along about October, when the game is nearly over. This means we work like dogs in the last quarter of the year, miss our goal, and feel bad about ourselves. We then equate setting goals with feeling bad and, understandably, say "to hell with goals."

The setting and achievement of goals need not be a mysterious and complex procedure. We simply have to understand the way our minds work and do things accordingly. Here are some ideas I've found useful. Try them, and you might find defining objectives easier and even fun.

SET GOALS THAT ARE WELL WITHIN REASON

Goal-setting is like taking a drive in a car. You can only plan as far as you can see. When you get there, you can see a little further, and so set a new goal. A person earning $25,000 per year and setting a goal of $50,000 is smoking the broom. He can't even conceive what $50,000 feels like. Then, when he doesn't achieve the objective, he feels like he's failed and quits setting goals. If you earn $25,000, try to get to $27,500. As soon as you get there, shoot for $30,000, *if that's what you want.* If all you want is $27,500, be happy. Who says you are obliged to keep expanding and extending your goals? Whose life is it, anyhow?

SET GOALS OFTEN

The shorter the term of the goal, the more real it becomes to the subconscious. More and more of our top achievers are coming out of the closet and stating publicly that they don't set goals. They actually believe this. Yet if you ask them to go to a meeting with you tomorrow, they'll say, "I'd love to, but I can't. I have a breakfast meeting, and an appointment at 10:00 A.M., then a lunch date and three quotations to get out." Wht are these, if they aren't goals?

Setting down long-term goals has proved to be of marginal benefit to me. As a young man, I used to set five-year goals, because I went to a seminar. After nearly twenty years of this, I was able to make some interesting observations. In retrospect, my five-year goals fell in roughly two categories: (1) those I had run past well before the five years had expired; (2) those I never achieved at all, because they had become unimportant to me, because *I had changed*.

We are growing, changing, thinking animals. I have no idea what I'll be doing in five years. Had you told me ten years ago that I'd be sitting here writing this book and flying around the world giving speeches, I'd have recommended competent psychiatric help. I had no intention of doing this, had no desire to do this, and felt I lacked the ability to do this. I would never have set this as a goal, yet here I am doing it and having the time of my life. Of what benefit are long-term goals?

Consider setting goals weekly, or monthly, or at most quarterly. If, in fact, you are growing and progressing, you'll need to update and change your goals frequently to keep them meaningful.

SET GOALS IN PRESENT TIME

The subconscious seems not to understand "I was" or "I'm going to be"; it only understands "*I am*." As opposed to saying, "I will earn $50,000 this year," try "I enjoy consistently earning at the rate of $50,000 per year." All you need is one $5,000 month and you're on schedule. Time to reexamine the goal.

Not, "I want to buy a new 450SL," but "I love the wind ruffling my hair as I drive my new 450SL."

The more vivid the imagery and the more closely it is related to present time, the quicker will be the reaction of our subconscious—which in turn will lead us to pursue the goal.

Now, this doesn't need to be a big deal. You don't need expensive systems, or thick books with lots of pages. A simple Daytimer™ or datebook will do just fine. I've seen many high producers survive very nicely using notepaper and the backs of envelopes. If it works for you, keep on doing it. Keep them simple, keep them clear, but *write them*.

I've found it effective to segregate my desires into two categories, "To Have" and "To Be."

"To Have" is a list of desired toys, or material things, I want to possess. A new home, a new car, new suits, a 1,000-c.c. motorcycle that'll climb trees and blow flame out the. back. Most of these things cost money and can have a specific value attached to them. Noting the value is important, as this clarifies the task for the subconscious.

Some things, like a house, I can't pay cash for, so I assign a monthly payment. Probably allowance also ought to be made for details like food, utilities, insurance, and taxes.

A "To Have" list might look a little like this (fill in your own numbers):

TO HAVE	COST
House payment	_____
Car payment	_____
Food	_____
Utilities	_____
Insurance	_____
Clothes	_____
Taxes	_____

Toy	_____
Toy	_____
Toy	_____
Toy	_____
Toy	_____
TOTAL "TO HAVE" COST	_____

It's important to get accurate values, as your subconscious won't believe you if you lie to it. It's also important to get the toys when you get the bucks. If you don't reward yourself, your subconscious will know you don't mean it and will ease off. Lots of toys are absolutely essential. Your subconscious is not very clear on money, but can get really involved with the toys money buys.

"To Be" is a list that may, or may not, have money values attached. This is a list of things you want to change *to be* a better person. Maybe a professional designation (cost), a private pilot (cost), a better parent (no cost), a better listener (no cost), or a better golfer (lots of cost). If, as an example, you decide to read a book a month, you'd better figure the cost of the books.

Please take a couple of minutes to write down some things you would like to be and the cost, if any. Don't fuss over this. If you change your mind, change your list. It's your list. Nobody's going to check your work.

TO BE	COST
_____	_____
_____	_____
_____	_____
_____	_____

_____	_____
_____	_____
_____	_____
_____	_____
_____	_____
_____	_____

TOTAL "TO BE" COST   _____

TOTAL NEEDED   _____

Now we have a really good reason to make money, a reason the subconscious can relate to—and that's important. Many people set a goal of $50,000 a year without needing it, or really without even knowing what they'd do with it if they got it. The subconscious doesn't understand it or believe it and won't go for it.

Let's assume, just for laughs, that your list came to $50,000 per year. (Wouldn't that be a fascinating coincidence?) You say, "O.K., subconscious, there's the target. Go get it." Your subconscious says, "Huh?" Here's the problem. Your subconscious, unaided, doesn't know *how* to make $50,000 a year. It needs a little more help from the conscious. Fifty thousand dollars is the result, and it's nearly impossible to manage results. Results, however, come from activity, which is a cinch to manage. We need to set *activity goals*, so our subconscious knows what to do when our feet hit the floor in the morning.

MANAGE ACTIVITY, NOT RESULTS

We need to know how many people we must see every day in order to achieve our objective. We're going to use a Sales Activity Calculator for this (see form on opposite page).

96

THE TRISLER COMPANY
SALES ACTIVITY CALCULATOR

This Sales Activity Calculator will enable you to determine the average number of contacts per day you must make to achieve your goal for the next twelve months.

Salesperson's name _____

1. Your average earnings per sale are . . . . _____

2. How much money do you want to earn in the next twelve months? . . . . _____

3. How many presentations do you make to gain a sale? . . . . _____

4. Divide your earnings per sale (1) by presentations per sale (3). This is your earnings per presentation . . . . _____

5. a. How many contacts do you make to gain a presentation? . . . . _____
   b. Divide your earnings per presentation (4) by contacts per presentation (5a). This is your earnings per contact . . . . _____

6. a. Divide your earnings goal for the next twelve months (2) by the number of weeks you will work. The result is weekly earnings . . . . . _____
   b. Divide the result by 5 or 6, depending on the number of working days. This is your earnings goal per day . . . . _____

7. Divide earnings per day (6b) by earnings per contact (5b). This is your required contacts per day to achieve your earnings goal . . . . _____

However, no form is really needed once you know how to arrive at the numbers.

Let's take an example of a Dooger salesperson whose "To Have" and "To Do" Lists (annualized) indicate a need for $50,000 over the next twelve months and work through the Sales Activity Calculator, step by step.

Step 1. Average earnings per sale can be gotten from the average of the salesperson's last ten pay vouchers, or commission checks. Yes, I know, your income swings widely. You're on straight commission. Or you're on salary plus bonus. No matter. Everyone has averages. They vary from time to time, but we all have averages. Find yours. Let's assume this person gets an *average* of $400 each time a Dooger sells.

Step 2. The "To Have" and "To Do" lists have revealed a need for $50,000 over the next twelve months.

Step 3. A presentation is defined as any time you get to tell your story to a qualified prospect. How do we know how many presentations it takes to make a sale? Keep primitive records. In your daily planning book, simply mark a P every time you make a presentation. If, at the end of the month you have 30 P's and have made 10 sales, it takes you an average of 3 presentations a sale. *Critical point:* Keep your own records. Don't use the averages of anyone else. Numbers will vary widely, according to the people involved, market conditions, and products sold. Clearly, as you progress and do a better job, your ratio of sales to presentations will improve. If your averages do not reflect reality, you won't believe them and this whole exercise will be a waste of time.

Let's assume the records of this Dooger salesperson show an average of 3 presentations per sale.

Step 4. Earnings per sale ($400) divided by presentations

per sale (3) means our Dooger salesperson earns $133.34 every time he makes a presentation, whether the customer buys or not. Now what does this do to our need for high pressure and power closing? The answer is very clear. We make $133.34 per presentation, whether the person says yes or no. The key, then, is to make more presentations, not just grind on the poor prospect we've got.

Step 5a. What constitutes a contact? Anytime we speak to a suspect and inquire as to his need for our product or service. "Hi, I'm Farley. Want to buy a Dooger?" Bingo. That's a contact. Anytime you surprise a customer, or he surprises you, that's a contact. If you like, you can even count phone calls and handwritten notes. Anytime you reach another human being, it's a contact. How do we find out how many it takes to yield a presentation? Primitive record-keeping. Every time we make a contact, we mark a / in our daily planner. At the end of the month, we have lots of 𝍱 𝍱 𝍱 𝍱.

Let's assume our Dooger salesperson has seen 450 people to get 30 presentations. This would seem to indicate an average of 15 contacts per presentation. Again, the usability of this plan will be no better than the quality of your numbers. Be straight with yourself.

Step 5b. We now divide our earnings per presentation ($133) by the contacts per presentation (15) to get $8.89 per contact. Let's round that off to $9, which is close enough for government work. "You mean I make $9 every time I hand out a card, whether or not they buy?" You got it. Could this realization make prospecting more fun? Every time we contact another warm body, we make money. The amount of money depends on your personal averages.

Step 6a. To find the necessary weekly income, divide the annual earnings goal ($50,000) by the number of weeks to be worked, say 50—which means we'll have to earn $1,000 per week, no small task. If you want more time off over the year, earn more per week.

Step 6b. Let's assume we only want to work 5 days a week. We now need to earn $200 per day.

Step 7. We now divide our needed earnings per day ($200) by our earnings per contact ($9) to find that we need to see 22 people every day to meet our goal.

"Wow," you say, "That's an awful lot of people to see." Fine. Here are your options.

1. Settle for less money.
2. Improve your ratio of presentations to sales.
3. Improve your ratio of contacts to presentations.
4. Sell something that gives you more money per sale.
5. Face reality and see 22 people.
6. Lie about the numbers, kid yourself, and flush out of selling. Figures don't lie, but liars can figure.

If you are aware of other options, please let me know.

The formula is infallible. The only time it will fall apart is when the numbers fed in are erroneous. In the computer business, they love to say "garbage in, garbage out," along with other droll remarks.

Manage activity, not results. If you don't know where you're going, how will you know when you're lost?

II

Selling Somebody

9
BEFORE IT'S TIME FOR YOU TO GO

*"Opportunity for distinction lies in doing
ordinary things well and not in erratically striving
to perform grandstand plays."*

—*William Feather*

The commonly promoted line on selling has been to clearly
delineate your goal, visualize yourself achieving your objective, make a positive affirmation of that objective, and
go out and smite them, hip and thigh. This thinking has
bred legions of salespeople whose concept of selling is to
run around giving their pitch and closing early, often, and
hard.

Bull. Positive affirmations and hard work are fine, as far
as they go, but we need additional planning to achieve op-
timal results. Let's examine this historical affirmation:

"I can whip all the Indians on the continent with the Seventh Cavalry."

General George Armstrong Custer emphatically deliv-
ered this statement prior to the Battle of Little Big Horn.

Did he have a clearly delineated goal? Seems pretty clear to me. He wanted to whup 'em. Was his attitude positive? Absolutely. He was going to run them over. You think maybe he didn't visualize himself, flaxen mane flowing, saber flashing, guns blazing, just flat kicking their butts?

According to the "company line," he had all the essential ingredients for success, but his research was incomplete. All the positive thinking and enthusiasm in the world won't save you if you don't do your homework. We need to spend some quiet time, alone, before each sales call to plan our approach and anticipate possible areas of conflict. We need to have not only a "success plan" but a "disaster plan." Many lost sales have been salvaged through effective damage control.

DETERMINE CALL OBJECTIVES

Have you ever noticed how much easier it is to make a sales call when you have just had a big sale? You're hot and oiled and ready to go. Everything just seems to fall into place. Conversely, isn't it the pits to try to go out again when you've just made a call and they set the dogs on you? The image of that recent failure looms large in your mind. You're positive all right. You're *positive* they won't buy. And they don't.

Wouldn't it be terrific if you never had to lose on a sales call again? If every time you went out, you had a "win"? Sounds too good to be true, doesn't it? Fairy tales can come true, it can happen to you, if you have a long enough list of call objectives. The only reason we lose, on most sales calls, is that we did not provide ourselves with enough opportunities to win.

I'm going to suggest you sit down before every sales call

and make a list of objectives, in descending order of importance. This will not only help you get a win on every sale, it'll help you remember what you're going out for.

Let's assume you're going out to sell a Dooger. Obviously, if you can sell Doogers, you can sell *anything*. We would make a list of call objectives that might look like this:

1. *Sell the Dooger.* This has probably never happened to you, but on occasion when going home from a sale I didn't make, I've recalled that I didn't ask them to buy. We just had a great time and a fine conversation, but they *didn't buy.* Nowadays, before I leave a customer, I glance at my list of objectives to see if I've covered this one. If I haven't explicitly asked him to buy, now's the time.

2. *Make another appointment.* If we can't get them in the boat this time, we'll try for another appointment. Many sales are made with the second effort.

3. *Get more information.* If we are unsuccessful in our efforts to make another appointment, we can, at least, dig for more information about the customer, his problems, and ways to help him solve those problems. These data can't help but serve us well in the future.

4. *Get referrals.* Maybe they don't want to buy our Dooger, but who do they know at work, in the neighborhood, in their club, who might enjoy owning one? Most buyers are not religiously opposed to Dooger-buying; they just don't want one. They'll be delighted to fink on their friends. It helps take the heat off them.

5. *Make a friend.* If all else fails, let's leave an atmosphere conducive to future dialogue.

Let's review our list of *written* objectives:

1. Sell the Dooger
2. Make another appointment
3. Get more information
4. Get referrals
5. Make a friend

Now honestly, out of a spread like that, can't we get at least one of them? This means that we'll never again "lose" on a sale; just some days we'll win bigger than others. This may strike you as a form of mental masturbation, but it really aids our sales efforts in two critical areas:

1. It provides clarity of purpose and direction.
2. It shields our fragile egos from the reality of failure.

DETERMINE CUSTOMER ATTITUDES

We need to spend time reflecting on customers and how they might react to us, and us to them. We've already discussed the fact that our customers are individuals and must be treated individually. Every customer you meet is different from every other customer you have met before. Our sales success will depend, in large measure, on our ability to relate to the widely divergent individuals we meet.

Jerry Richardson, in his fine book *The Magic of Rapport*, outlines a basic law of human relations, called The Law of Requisite Variety:

"In any system, the individual with the widest range of responses will control the system."

Here's where the "canned pitch" falls apart; it does not provide for the individuality of our customers. You can be the finest country singer in the world, but if your customer wants opera, you're in trouble. You can bake the world's greatest apple pie, but if your customer wants huckleberry, you're out of business.

If you can answer more questions than the customer can ask, you'll win. If you can find a way to flow with the customer through varying moods and emotions, you'll go away with a sale and a new friend.

Although people are individual and cannot be handily categorized, there are some broad categories of human behavior, and sales strategies appropriate to these categories. Let's examine four types of buyers you have probably encountered and some effective methods of dealing with them.

Sheila Shriek

Shriekers initially strike terror into the hearts of salespeople, particularly new ones. They are distrustful, overbearing, and argumentative. They love to be in control and would far rather fight than switch. They'll argue any side of a question, just for the pure joy of arguing. They are belligerent and aggressive. They are insensitive. If you say to a shrieker, "I've got a problem. I think my kid's smoking dope," he'll reply, "Here's a dime. Call somebody who gives a damn."

Their insensitivity leads to total inflexibility. They don't know what you think and couldn't care less. There's a poem that goes:

> In controversial moments,
>   my perception's rather fine.
> I always see both points of view,
>   the one that's wrong and mine.

Shriekers are filled with strong negative emotions and are eager to share these feelings with those around them. They believe that all salespeople are corrupt and totally unnecessary. If your stuff was any good, they'd sell it in vending machines, or by mail order. Who needs you?

They believe the only way to deal with salespeople is to stay in control, which they do by yelling, accusing, bullying, and generally comporting themselves in abominable fashion. Shriekers revel in their image as people who are tough to do business with, but they're not so tough. Their inflexibility makes them easily dealt with by a salesperson who understands The Law of Requisite Variety.

Never argue with a shrieker. They love to fight and hate to lose. Even if you win the argument, you lose because they'll hate you for it.

Allow Sheila to vent strong negative emotions. These folks are just brimming with bad feelings about salespeople in general, and often you in particular. Let them blow off steam. As soon as the pressure is relieved, they'll feel better and be much easier to reason with. Don't argue, just listen.

Probe flat statements. Shriekers often make statements such as: "All you salespeople are *thieves.*" There is a temptation, on our part, to take umbrage with this sort of tack. To do so will put us right where the shrieker wants us—in the middle of a fight. We might be more effective with something like, "You must have had a bad experience to make you feel that way. Would you tell me about it?" The shrieker will normally dump his bucket and feel much better.

Be firm. If shriekers love anything more than a fight, it's bullying someone. If they feel they can push you around, they'll push you right out of the state. Saint Ambrose wrote, "Neither give offense to others, nor take offense from them."

108

Shriekers admire strength as long as it doesn't threaten them. Argument breeds more argument. If we merely listen carefully, while maintaining our integrity and composure, they'll get the message. The fine old sales trainer Elmer Wheeler once said, "People seldom want to walk over you until you lie down."

Morton Morose

Morton generally appears a bit depressed. He is very secretive and unresponsive. Questions are often answered with grunts or shrugs. He seems aloof and wary. Often he looks at you out of the corner of his eye, while he puffs on his pipe.

If you run a "canned pitch" on him, he'll listen disinterestedly, then tell you he wants to think it over. You'll never hear from him again.

Morton is afraid you're going to take advantage of him. His primary method of dealing with salespeople is avoidance. He'll be late for appointments, or entirely absent. You'll get no conversation you don't dig for. I've heard him described as a "fish."

Go slow with Morton. If we dance into his life with bubbling enthusiasm and silver-tongued patter, we'll be acting exactly as he thought we were going to act and he'll pull deeper into his shell, like a turtle. We have to reassure him that we're different, that we are not going to "pitch" and "power-close" him. High pressure is totally ineffective on a turtle.

Probe Morton. We can't establish trust unless we can involve him through probing and heavy use of pauses. If we give him a chance, he'll talk and we can guide him to a good decision. Remember, he who talks dominates the conversation; he who listens controls the conversation.

This person wants to be loved. Motormouths are happy, enthusiastic, warm people who are fun to be with. They love to see you coming and will regale you with countless stories, jokes, and pictures of relatives. Everybody enjoys and likes them because they try to please everyone. They are willing to trust, give in readily, and, as a result, are exploited by aggressive people. They prefer small talk and will avoid getting down to business.

It takes a long time to sell Marion, as she keeps going off on side tracks. If we "power-close" her, she'll find a very plausible reason—one "obviously" beyond her control—to cancel the order.

Love them. Their primary motivator is love. If you love them, they'll love you and you'll do business.

Listen to them. Allow them to tell you stories. Laugh at their jokes, but gently guide the conversation back to the central business matter.

Avoid pressuring. If they feel they're being manipulated, they'll interpret that as a lack of love and they'll be hurt. When hurt, they won't buy from you.

Avoid technical data. Don't drown these highly emotional people with lots of graphs and details. They'll doze off. Give just enough facts to justify their emotional reaction.

Terry Tycoon

Terry is penetrating, frank, and businesslike. As opposed to being loved by associates and peers, the term most often used to describe Terry is "respected."

He'll strive for mutual understanding and full disclosure. He's willing to listen and learn and will analyze your proposal very carefully. An open, honest, intimate relationship is easily established with Terry.

Know your facts. Terry has an excellent B.S. detector and will readily see through an ill-prepared presentation. Know your competition, and use this knowledge. You can bet he knows about your competition. Deal in specifics whenever possible. Don't say "the biggest," say exactly how big.

Be organized, yet flexible. A razzle-dazzle pitch will destroy you. Know the benefits of your plan, but be open to messages from Terry. Be ready to move on quickly, as he bores readily.

Emphasize innovation. People buy for only two reasons: hope of gain, or fear of loss. Sheila, Morton, and Marion will tend to buy more from fear of loss. With them, we emphasize stability, proven performance, and the idea that things will remain pretty much as they are. Terry will buy for hope of gain. With him, we show that our product or service is on the leading edge of technology.

IDENTIFY TENTATIVE NEEDS

Since people buy for their reasons, not ours, it is nearly impossible to determine the needs of a customer until he tells us what he thinks he needs. We can, however, review our knowledge of the customer to try to anticipate areas of need.

How have other people benefited from our product or service? Why might this particular customer need our product or service?

PLAN THE CONTACT

"Canned pitches" don't work, but we'd better have a good idea of what's going to happen during the first five minutes, or we'll be in deep trouble. If the first five minutes go well, the rest of the interview seems to flow along too, but if you get buried at the outset, the rest of the call will be like swimming in Cream of Wheat.

This may seem rather basic, but *be sure your product works*. I have seen countless sales blown because the salesperson's demonstrator was functioning improperly, or not at all, or the salesperson *didn't know how to run the thing*.

I have been in the market for a word processor lately. I know nothing about computers, so I went to a word processing show at the Convention Center to get an overview. One highly advertised national brand, let's call it Sentence Master, seemed to fit our needs nicely. We asked the booth attendant for a demonstration. He explained that it was a new model, and that since he was in management, he didn't know how to run it. Having been a sales manager myself, I could understand his position. He said he'd have a salesman call me.

About a month later, after having looked at seven other competing systems, I decided to call the Sentence Master people again. You see, one of the competing salespeople had told me that his machine was overqualified for my needs, but the Sentence Master was just perfect. The people at Sentence Master assured me they hadn't forgotten me, they'd just been busy. The salesman said he'd be out in a week to evaluate our needs. *Good!*

I chatted with the Sentence Master man for nearly an hour, telling more than I knew about our needs. We made an appointment for 1:30 the next afternoon, at his office for a demonstration. He was a nice young man. I decided to take along a company check to facilitate purchase, as my mind was 98 percent made up.

Promptly at 1:30 P.M., I arrived at his office, flushed with the glow of buying fever. And—*the damn thing wouldn't work*. He got another Sentence Master, and *it wouldn't work either*. He was terribly embarrassed and explained that he normally checked the machines out prior to demonstration, but he'd been busy. I understand his position, but it sounds like a personal problem to me. This book is being written with a pencil, as I have not yet bought a word processor. When I do, it sure as hell won't be a Sentence Master.

Whatever we're selling, let's make sure the demonstrator is spotless and works flawlessly.

10
HOW TO MAKE EACH TIME LIKE THE FIRST TIME, ONLY LAST LONGER

"Anybody can win—unless there happens to be a second entry."

—George Ade

As we just discussed, your first five minutes will shape the balance of your sales call. Let's look at the factors that go into making a great first five minutes.

BE ON TIME

No single act can so totally destroy our credibility as tardiness. It shows a total lack of respect for time—our time and the customer's time. Vince Lombardi, the renowned football coach, wore a watch set twenty minutes early. If you got to an appointment with him five minutes early, you were already fifteen minutes *late*. All his players learned to live on "Lombardi time." It's far better to wait for your customer a few minutes, because you are early, than to have your customer wait for you for a few seconds, because you're late. Besides, if you're prompt, you'll have one less thing to apologize for, which leads us to point two:

NEVER APOLOGIZE

I don't care what goes wrong, *never apologize*. Apologies only draw the customer's attention to the problem. If we don't bring it up, he may not notice.

A number of years ago, I participated in a sales conference at the Shrine Auditorium in San Diego. I was to open the program at 8:30 A.M., so was there by 7:00 A.M., just to be on the safe side. I hadn't done a lot of public speaking and was therefore very excited and more than a little nervous. A cardinal rule of public speaking is to go to the men's room *before* the program, so you won't go *during* the program. Accordingly, at 8:15 A.M., I dutifully made the pilgrimage.

Denim suits were all the rage then, and I had a beauty. A brand new Raphael dark blue denim with flared jacket and slacks. I was a veritable fashion plate. While in the men's room, I noticed my glasses were filthy so I decided to wash them so I could see out. Unprepared for the water pressure in the Shrine Auditorium, I shoved my glasses under the faucet and hit the valve. The glasses served as a fine deflector, protecting the sink from dampness and squirting about a quart of water on the front of my new denim slacks.

Did you ever see how water looks on denim? Let me just

say it's noticeable. I was completely panicked. How was I ever going to explain this? Who'd believe me if I did?

I was standing in the parking lot of the Shrine Auditorium, facing the sun, my slacks stuffed with paper towels, when my old friend Cavett Robert strolled up. "What is it you're doing?" he inquired. I breathlessly explained my predicament and sobbed, "What am I going to tell them?"

He said, "Don't tell them anything. Never tell people your troubles. Eighty percent of them don't care, and the other 20 percent are actually *glad*."

That's some of the best advice I ever got. I did my job, and maybe no one noticed. If they did, *they* sure weren't going to bring up the subject.

DEVELOP RAPPORT

How do you get someone to like you? Say "Please like me"? I think not. Dale Carnegie, in his book *How to Win Friends and Influence People*, wrote, "You can make more friends in two months by becoming really interested in other people, than you can in two years by trying to get other people interested in you."

Listen to your customers and chat with them about the subject in which they have the most interest, themselves. The more they talk about themselves, the more they'll like you. "Tell me, how did you happen to get started in this business?" This simple question is often good for half an hour, or better, of unilateral conversation.

In Chapter 3, we discussed speaking at the same rate as our customer. That's important, but not nearly as important as listening. Fred Herman, in a sales seminar I attended many years ago, said:

His thoughts were slow,
his words were few
and never formed a glisten,
But he was a joy
whenever he called.
You should have heard him
listen.

STATE YOUR PURPOSE

Let's tell them, up front, why we're there. The next guy who comes to my home, telling me that my home has been selected as a model for complimentary siding, is going to get his face ripped off. He really wants to sell me siding, so let him *say so.* Any relationship that starts out based on a lie is bound to fail.

"I'm here to discuss how your home can be marketed."

"Let's take a ride in a Belchfire 4. I hope you'll want to own one."

"I'm here to show you how you can benefit from owning a new Dooger."

A clear-cut statement of purpose removes any possibility of subterfuge or misunderstanding. It's a courtesy we owe to our customers. Honesty not only is the best policy, it's sufficiently rare these days to make you pleasantly conspicuous.

A couple of weeks ago, I was discussing word processors with a friend of mine, the Vice President of Sales and Marketing for a large electronics company. He had just purchased a brand I'll call Phrase-O-Matic and was awaiting delivery. I asked him if he had considered a Sentence Master. His answer was enlightening. He said, "Yes, we looked at a Sentence Master. They dropped their price more every time we talked to them. By the time we bought, they were $12,000 under Phrase-O-Matic. We never knew what the *real* price was. Every time we asked a question, the Sentence Master man had an answer, often wrong. The woman selling the Phrase-O-Matic often said she didn't know, but could find out. In our final decision meeting, that $12,000 price differential looked awfully good, but we felt the salesman was flaky."

The woman from Phrase-O-Matic overcame a $12,000 price disadvantage with truth, the most powerful selling tool of all.

MAKE AN INITIAL BENEFIT STATEMENT

Make an *initial benefit statement* at the beginning of the presentation. This gives a couple of general benefits of owning the product, then the advantages of our specific product. Examples:

"Most folks want to be sure they have enough money put aside to really enjoy retirement. Our 'Bucks-A-Plenty' individual retirement account gives high return with maximum safety, and it's all tax sheltered."

"People in your field tell me that on-time delivery, high quality, and competitive price make their jobs easier. Our new Super Dooger can be in your shop within 15 days of order, has a 98 percent acceptance rate, and is priced right."

An initial benefit statement gets the ball rolling. If our first five minutes go smoothly, we're well on our way to a satisfied customer.

11
GETTING TO KNOW YOU

"I don't have opinions. I only try to communicate the opinions of others attractively."

—Dr. Henry Kissinger

While "canned pitches" don't work, they're still in wide use. Ever wonder why? We're afraid of silence. If we appear before a customer and don't say anything, that's all right, unless the customer also doesn't say anything. Then it could get *very quiet*, and that's bad. The 80–20 rule of selling, whereby the customer talks 80 percent of the time, is really terrific, but many of our customers are unaware of the rule. They convey their lack of awareness by the statement, "O.K., come on in and give me your pitch." Ever hear that one? They are saying, in effect, "Me Customer—I listen. You Salesperson—you talk." That's the way they've been trained to act by salespeople encountered in their past. If we immediately start to babble, we'll be right back in the old "canned pitch" mold.

People buy for their reasons, not ours, so we have to diagnose before we can prescribe. Feedback is absolutely essential for selling today. Without feedback, we're a cannonball roaring toward a target that may well have moved. Feedback lets us be a heat-seeking missile. Wherever the target goes, we can follow. Here are a few methods for getting feedback.

Tell them you want feedback. People treat us the way we have trained them to treat us. If you don't like the treatment, change the training. Many of our customers have been trained, by salespeople, to sit quietly and listen to "the pitch." When they say, "Give me your pitch," let's tell them, "I really don't have a pitch. Let's see whether I can help *you* solve *your* problem." Then let's ask them questions which will cause their needs to become apparent, to us and to them.

Use silence to encourage feedback. Nature abhors a vacuum. Silence is a form of vacuum. Words will always rush in to fill a silence. If they're our words, we lose. Whenever we ask a question, we must shut up long enough for the customer to send an answer. In the case of Morton Morose, this may take some time, but shut up anyhow.

Watch nonverbal responses. We can get hordes of input from what our customers *don't* say. If a customer puts her head down on her arms, this may indicate a lack of interest in our presentation.

Many fine books have been written on kinesics, body language, or nonverbal communication. There are problems, however, whenever we try to oversimplify this very complex subject. Some authors feel that if I cross my arms and legs, I'm rejecting you. On the other hand, I may just be cold or have to go to the bathroom.

As opposed to trying to read too much into specific gestures, let's be aware of *changes* in body language. If a person suddenly leans back, or stops making eye contact, the communication line may well have broken. When this happens, stop talking. The customer will usually start. That's right, just stop, right in the middle of your sent-. . . . Your customer probably won't even notice you didn't finish the sentence. He was thinking about what he was going to say when it was his turn to talk. You stopped. The silence indicates it's his turn to talk, and off he will go.

If the customer isn't listening, why talk?

The next way to get feedback is to *use nondirective probes*. In Chapter 2 we discussed the valuable words "who," "where," "what," "why," "when," and "how." In our effort to discover needs, these are the finest tools we have. The real beauty of nondirective probes is that they're so easy to remember. "Canned pitches" are hard to remember, and if you lose your place, you're in real trouble.

The above list of words is by no means complete. One of the finest, and shortest, nondirective probes I have ever heard is "Oh?" Now what do you do when someone says "Oh?" to you? You tend to explain further, don't you? So do I.

A couple of years ago, I was sitting in my office at about 10:00 o'clock in the morning. I wasn't hurting anybody. I wasn't doing anybody much good either. I was just sitting there. Ever have a day like that? Actually, I was making a chain out of paper clips. That's good therapy—keeps your hands away from your nose.

My secretary was out making the second pot of coffee and was not there to protect me. This nattily attired man appeared before my desk, and, reading the nameplate on my desk (I have a sign on my desk so I know where to sit), said, "Mr. *Trizeler*, I'm offering to businessmen in this area a new Non-Can Disability Policy."

I didn't like this guy much. Not only did he mispronounce my name, but I didn't even know what a Non-Can Disability Policy was. I finally figured out that it was insurance, and that clinched it. I don't like insurance. I don't like any deal where you have to get sick or die to win. As a result, I'm not real crazy about insurance salesmen, and I shared this information with him.

He said: "Oh?"

I thought: "O.K., Moosebreath. If you're looking for rejection, you just found the depot." And I proceeded to give him a truckload of abuse.

He said: "Oh, you must have had a terrible experience to cause you to feel that way. Would you tell me about it?"

Me: "Blah blah blah blah. . . ."

Every so often, when I'd start to slow down, he'd throw in another "Oh?" or "Oh, tell me more." *I did.* He kept me talking for the better part of 45 minutes. Did you ever try to talk for 45 minutes about *disability insurance?* I defy you to do so without repeating yourself several times. Every time I repeated myself, it sounded just a little dumber than it did the preceding time. I was boring myself and getting cramps in front of my ears from running my mouth so much.

When I finally ground to a halt, exhausted, he said, "Now just to help me clarify my thinking . . ." and I *knew* I was in trouble. I believe the greatest sales presentations I have ever witnessed are nonverbal, where very few words are passed by the salesperson. This guy was a master. I like to think I've got a nice, comfortable office, and this guy looked all around it, very slowly. I looked too, to see what he was looking at. He looked at my fireplace, my coffee table, my paintings, and my ego wall. (Oh sure, I have got an ego wall, just like you do. All seasoned salespeople have them. It's covered with plaques, diplomas, and certificates. Among other things, I have my schoolboy patrol certificate from the seventh grade. When I'm having a bad day, I can go to the wall and put my face up against those plaques. They're cool and remind me of when people loved me.) Upon completion of his obviously approving inspection, he said, "Now just to help me clarify my thinking, are you telling me you cannot afford the $17 monthly premium, or are you saying you don't plan to become sick or injured?"

I was the proud new owner of a Non-Can Disability Policy. Did he need 75 closes? No way. He simply used the nondirective probe "Oh?" to cause me to run my mouth until I had built a fence so high, I couldn't jump over it. Then he just strolled over and shut the gate. I had no choice.

The next point is to *reward feedback*. There is no such thing as bad feedback. Oh, we may, on occasion, get some feedback we'd just as soon not have heard. Sometimes someone, heaven forfend, will even hurt our feelings, but aren't we better off knowing what he thinks? When we know what the problem is, we can then choose to try to solve it, or, if we can't, terminate the relationship.

Whenever we get feedback, let's think, "That's *good*, now we're getting somewhere"—and thank them for sharing their thoughts. Never argue. If we argue, we'll take great strides toward eliminating feedback altogether. People, other than Sheila Shriek, don't really like to argue. If we continue to press the point, they may well just shut up and let us babble on. We *lose*.

Malcolm Forbes, the publisher of *Forbes* magazine, once said, "A bore is someone who persists in holding to his own view after we have enlightened him with ours."

Here's a challenge. Out of all the things people say to us, we have to sort out those needs which are really important to them. This requires *active listening* at the highest level. We should periodically rephrase and summarize what they're saying to us to be sure we understand clearly.

Taking notes is an essential and seldom performed function. An old Arab proverb says, "The strongest memory is weaker than the palest ink." If we don't write down those needs important to the customer, we, being human, will forget them and talk about those needs *we* think should be important. *People buy for their reasons, not ours.*

If taking notes seems stilted, or unnatural, consider a phrase like this. "You're going to be saying some very important things to me. I want to be sure I don't forget any. Do you mind if I take notes?" Will they mind? Hell, no. How long has it been since anyone told you you were going to say something important? Well, they haven't heard it in a long time either, and they'll be *delighted* to have you take notes. In fact, once they've become accustomed to the idea, they may help you. If you miss something, a customer may say, "Hey, you missed that, and that's *important.*" This list of needs that are important to the customer will be very valuable when it comes time to close.

COMPARE NEEDS WITH INITIAL ASSUMPTIONS

Before we met the customer, we made a list of needs he *might* have. Now comes the test of our flexibility. We compare the needs the customer thinks he has with the needs we thought he'd have. If these lists do not align, we must *revise our assumptions.*

It is far more important to make the sale than to be "right." We don't really care why they buy, as long as they *buy*.

When our revision is complete, we must now summarize the customer's position, as we see it, and:

GAIN AGREEMENT ON NEEDS

We cannot go on to the next step until clear agreement on the customer's perception of his needs is reached. We now summarize and rephrase until the customer finally says, "Yes, that's it. That's what I need." As long as the customer continues to say, "No, that's not right. Let me put it this way. . . ." we haven't got it. Let's listen carefully, then play it back again until an agreement is achieved.

In selling, the pay is far greater for *asking the right questions* than for *knowing the right answers*. People don't care how much you know until they know how much you *care* about them.

12
LET ME SHOW YOU HOW IT WORKS

"No one can give faith unless he has faith. It is the persuaded who persuade."

—Joseph Joubert

When, and *only* when, we and the customer are in alignment as to what the customer's problems are, we can show how our product or service can solve those problems. Agreement on needs is critical, as if we don't know what the customer wants, we'll try to tell him what he *should* want. I believe the second greatest enemy of the salesperson of today is *talking about things that don't interest the customer.*

A few years ago, I decided I should own a Mercedes-Benz 450SL. Now, you've read their ads. You know why people buy a Mercedes-Benz. It has good brakes. It has ventilated disc brakes on all four wheels. You can cut the brake line to any of those wheels, and the other three will still work well. That's important, because that happens a lot. A Mercedes-Benz has four-wheel independent suspension. This means you can take that car out on a wet airstrip and slalom it around those red cones, like they do on TV, and you won't knock any down. That's important, because we all do that a lot. A Mercedes-Benz benefits from the highest-quality construction standards and state-of-the-art aerodynamic design. Did you know that when you drive a Mercedes-Benz in the rain, the airflow blows all the water off the side windows for optimum visibility? Yup. And that waste water is channeled through little grooves and gutters to the rear of the car where that waste water is used to *scrub* the taillights. That's why you buy a Mercedes-Benz. Must be so; that's what they say in their ads.

Bull! You buy a Mercedes-Benz so you can have little motors roll up your windows (you can't crank, might hurt yourself), turn on the air and stereo, and say, "I wonder what the *poor* folks are doing tonight." You buy a Mercedes-Benz to help you feel good about yourself.

I was an extra-motivated buyer. I had the "hardly waits." See, I had been driving a Porsche, but it had got all short. Got stuck in the side of a Cadillac. I had gone down to Avis to rent a car. They didn't have any cars, so they rented me a Dodge. You ever drive a Dodge? Nobody ought to have to drive one. It was a monkey vomit green four-door Polara. A slag heap on wheels. I didn't get an owner's manual, so I couldn't even figure out where to put the corn in that *hog*. I could "hardly wait" to get out of that sled and into a Mercedes-Benz.

I went down to the local Mercedes-Benz dealership, which seemed like a good place to start, and was cordially greeted by a salesman. I could tell he was a salesman, because he said, "Hep ya?"

I said, "Yeah. I've been thinking about buying a new Mercedes-Benz 450SL."

He said, "Great. What can I tell you about them?"

I said, "Well, I dunno. How fast do they go?"

He said, "Why is that important? You can only drive 55 anyhow."

Well, now, maybe *he* could only drive 55, but *I* could go like a bat out of hell and I had traffic tickets to prove it. I did what you'd probably have done. I took a brochure and went home to study. I didn't want to flunk any more tests.

In reading that brochure, I found that a Mercedes-Benz 450SL has K-Jetronic *Fuel Injection. Wow!* That must be fast. They wouldn't dare call it K-Jetronic unless it was fast, would they?

I went down again the next day and went through another door. I didn't want to meet the law-abiding-citizen salesman again. Another guy glided up and said, "Hep ya?"

I said, "Yeah. I've been thinking about a 450SL. The brochure said it has K-Jetronic Fuel Injection." (I could just *see* all those little German nozzles squirting gas into those cylinders, flame blasting out the back about four feet, driving the birds out of the trees.)

He said, "Yes sir. You can drive this car at 17,000 feet above sea level all day long. She'll never miss a lick."

Well now, the last time I checked, San Jose, where this discussion was taking place, was about 250 feet above sea level. I said, "I don't do a whole lot of that."

Undaunted, he riposted, "Well then, you'll be *delighted* to know about the fuel economy. This little beauty will give you 16 miles to the gallon around town, on *Regular* gas. It'll burn anything you can pump through a pipe."

I wasn't exactly delighted. If I was going to spend all that money on a 450SL, I sure didn't care about gas mileage. I wanted it to use enough gas so I wouldn't forget it was there. Besides, how fast can a car be that runs on *regular*? I wanted something that burned nitro in huge gulps. I don't know much about cars, but I have owned a few and I knew this much. The more gas they use, the faster they go. I wanted something with a five gallon toilet up under the hood. I could flush it with my foot and *whoooosh!!!*

I said, "I really don't care about gas mileage all that much."

He said, "Haven't you heard about the *energy crisis?* It's your patriotic *duty* to save fuel. Don't be *fuelish*." Then he took a little American flag out of his pocket and waved it at me.

What he didn't know about me was that I took physics in high school. They told us about a guy named Einstein and his $E = mc^2$ formula. He didn't realize he was dealing with an educated man. I don't remember how to do the formula, but I do remember one reason why it was important. There is as much energy available on the face of the earth today as there was a million years ago. It doesn't go away, it just changes form and converts to mass. Therefore, I conclude, there is no energy crisis. We have scads of energy. We have solar, wind, wave, tidal action, geothermal, hydroelectric, hydrogen, yes, even nuclear. We were just a little light on oil at the time. Even the most casual student of history understands that oil is but a passing fad. We didn't even use oil until 1900. In 1890, the first oil well on the North American continent was drilled in Pennsylvania. Prior to that time, we used whale oil. A funny thing happened. The whales got offended, and the price went up. We only use petroleum today because the price of whale oil is too high.

That's the way it works in a free-market society. As supply dwindles, price increases. When the price gets high enough, alternative energy sources become attractive.

Therefore, the solution to freeing ourselves from dependence on imported oil must be crystal clear to any educated person. *Use up that oil as fast as we can,* and I want to do my part.

Now this may sound ridiculous to you—it sure did to him—but bear in mind whose money was going into that Mercedes-Benz. I took another brochure and left him slowly shaking his head.

In the ensuing days, I made several visits to the dealership. One guy opened the door of that beautiful, fragile little roadster and bounced up and down on the open door to show me how well it was built. They must teach 'em that at Mercedes-Benz school. If anyone ever did that to *my* car, I'd punch out their lights. Another fellow showed me how the ashtray was mounted on ball bearings. Nobody seemed to care about me.

On my sixth visit to that dealership, the dealer came out of the back room, where he hides, and said, "You've been hanging around here a lot lately."

I said, "Yeah. I've been trying to justify the price of a 450SL. They sure cost a lot of money, you know."

He said, "Yeah, they *do* cost a lot of money, don't they?"

Something very different was happening from my previous visits. This guy was *agreeing* with me. In all my visits, this was the first person not to tell me what a fool I was for wanting what I wanted. I liked him a little already.

He inquired, "Why do you think you'd want a Mercedes-Benz anyhow?"

I said, "Well, I'm told they're fast."

He grinned, "*DAMN*, are they fast."

I yelled, "*Oh, good!* How fast are they?"

He said, "I can't tell you that. We don't conduct top speed tests anymore, but they go like a boiled owl."

I panted, "It says 160 miles per hour on the speedometer. Will it go *that* fast?"

He said, "Not with me in it, it won't, my friend."

I pleaded, "How fast have you had yours up to?"

He said, "I can't tell you that. You might be an officer of the law."

I whined, "I'm not a cop. Cross my heart and hope to die. *Please* tell me how fast you've gone in yours."

He said, "I really shouldn't, you promise you won't tell?"

I cried, "Oh God, yes. I promise."

He crooned, "That's good, because I have a position in this community to uphold. Besides that, I almost never drive when I've been drinking. It was a couple-three weeks ago and I'd been to a dealers' meeting in San Francisco. It was three o'clock in the morning, and I was coming home alone on Freeway 280. Big full moon, top down, wind blowing through what hair I've got left. I felt just like I was sixteen again. You know that long, straight stretch back of Palo Alto, by Page Mill Road?"

With eyes like dinner plates, I breathed, "Oh yeah. I know that stretch."

He continued, "Well I came under the Sand Hill overpass and looked down that long stretch. I saw no headlights or taillights, and I thought, 'What the hell, let's see what she'll do.' I just wrapped my toes around the radiator and hung on. Now I don't know how fast that car'll run, 'cause I ran out of guts before it ran out of go, but at the end of that stretch I was showing 135 miles an hour. I grinned so big I still have bugs in my teeth."

I whispered, "A hundred thirty-five miles an hour? Really? Oh that's *good*."

He said, "If you were to own a Mercedes-Benz, what color do you think you'd want?"

I said, "I don't really care. My wife picks the color. I've

always been partial to silver, but color's not really important to me."

He said, "*Silver*. Now I'm not a believer in fate, but you're not gonna believe what just happened. Just yesterday, the transport dropped off, in my back lot, a *silver* 450SL roadster. It has two tops and . . . you aren't allergic to leather, are you?"

Eagerly I cried, "Oh God, no. Look, I've got shoes on and everything. I *love* leather."

He said, "Oh, that's a relief. You've been reading all the brochures, and you know the standard upholstery on a 450SL is vinyl. Now it's good vinyl, the best available. Has holes poked in it to keep down sweating and all. It's plenty good enough for *most* people, but just based on the off chance that I might encounter a particularly discriminating individual, such as yourself, I took the liberty of ordering this one with top-grain *Austrian cowhide* upholstery. Would you like to see that car?"

He could probably tell, as I had begun drooling on my lapel. As we previously discussed, the finest sales presentations I have ever seen are non-verbal, where few, if any, words are passed. This guy was another master. He went over to a board and got the keys to that roadster. Together we waltzed to the back lot, where that lovely piece of work regally reposed. It had been sitting all day in 90° heat. You know what new cars smell like when they've been left sitting in the sun? Another example of government hype. The government tells you that that smell is nitrosamines—it comes out of the upholstery and the spare tire—and is supposed to kill you. That's the way I want to go.

He snuggled up close to that car, put the key in the door, and opened it about two inches. He hung his nose over the edge of the door glass and sniffed delicately—just stood there for about a month. I danced behind him, balanced on tippy toes, trying to avoid physical contact, which I felt would be rude. I wanted to get in that car so badly my teeth itched.

He pulled the door fully open and, with a broad and gracious sweep of his arm, indicated that my entrance to the sacred interior would be completely acceptable. I jammed my head and shoulders into that magnificent teutonic cocoon and, flaring my nostrils, hyperventilated on nitrosamines. I'm *so* glad that car was new. Had it been used, I'd have sucked the entire contents of the ashtray right up my nose.

Solemnly, he said, "Sixteen prime Austrian steers gave their *lives* for your comfort."

It took him less than a half hour to separate me from the full purchase price of that car. In fact, I paid $1,000 *more* than I had ever dreamed I would. I had to get special wheels to go with those leather seats. Did he need 75 closes? Certainly not. He said, "Press hard, the fourth copy's yours." I hesitated and looked at him for reassurance. Was I really doing the right thing? He comforted me, "You like it. You want it. You can afford it. *Buy it!*" I did.

THE SUPPORT CONCEPT

This Mercedes-Benz dealer employed the cornerstones of effective selling:

- Support those statements made by the customer which take us closer to our sales goal.
- Withhold support from those statements made by the customer which take us away from our sales goal.

The Mercedes-Benz dealer probed me to find areas of need, or dissatisfaction with my present status. When I said I wanted a fast car, he agreed with me and told me his car was fast. He stroked my ego and let me know it was O.K. to want what I wanted, and he was going to help me get it.

When I brought up a problem, price as an example, he withheld support. He didn't argue, he just flowed with me. I said, "They sure cost a lot of money."

He said, "Yeah, they *do* cost a lot of money, don't they?"

There's nothing for me to fight with in that statement. He's obviously on *my side*. Had he tried to tell me why I was wrong and why the car was worth the money, I would have had to defend my position. In so doing, I'd have sold myself more solidly on the fact that price was a problem. As it was, the question of price never came up again. I was *afraid* to mention price. He might have thought I couldn't afford it and not let me have it.

There are very few things we can say about *all* people. We are individuals. There is one common need in all of us, however: we all need *support*. Everyone needs physical and psychological support. We need someone to let us know it's all right to be who we are and want what we want. We need people to agree with us and make a fuss over us. The need for support exists in us from the day we are born and may have to do with the trauma of birth itself. You remember what *that* was like, don't you. You don't? Well, I'll refresh your memory, as I'm gifted with total recall.

I had been going along for nine months, give or take a few weeks. Everything was going pretty well. It was dark, no bright lights. It was quiet, no loud sounds, everything sort of muffled. It was warm, no drafts. (I hate drafts.) It was soft, with no sharp things poking me. I was doing well, just sitting and sucking my thumb, all creature comforts cared for. I was not anticipating any major change.

Then the wheels came off. I was outside, on a cold steel table. There's no cold like steel cold. There were brilliant lights blinding my pink little eyes. There were loud noises, people yelling and screaming, one of them being *me*. Then it got worse. A big fool in a white jumpsuit yanked me upside down and *beat on me*. I was distressed. People are always telling me of the joys of being "born again," but for this old boy, once was enough. Then . . . *the unkindest cut of all.* . . .

I was convinced that being born was the pits.

Except, now comes the good part. Nurses wrapped me in a blanket and fussed over me. "Look at all that *hair*. Looks like a monkey." "Is that a boy or a girl?" Gender proof was produced, and I was the center of attention. This was *fine*. I was being cooed at, cuddled, and generally catered to. I remember my Dad was so happy. He said, "Can I hold the baby?" He did. He said, "Let's name him Henry Jr." They did. He said, "Look, dear, Hank Jr.'s got my smile." Mom said, "You're holding him upside down."

From that day forward I've been addicted to support. So are our customers. Supporting is one of the best tools in selling today. And don't forget about nonsupport. In the absence of support from us, most of the objections we encounter will simply go away.

SELLING'S A.B.C.'s

As we demonstrate how our product or service will fulfill the customer's needs, let's bear in mind the A.B.C.'s of selling:

<u>A</u>dvantage. A product or service feature.

Benefit. What's in it for me? How will this feature solve my problem and improve my life?

Commitment. Agreement, on the part of the customer, that this advantage will truly benefit him.

Let's see how this might work for us in the real world.

"(A) This car has electronic fuel injection, (B) which means you'll not only have great fuel economy, but an extremely responsive engine under all weather and load conditions. (C) How does that sound?"

"(A) The house is located in the Grundoon Heights school district. (B) There, your children will have the finest education available in the state. (C) Your children's education is important to you, isn't it?"

"(A) Our Doogers are of the highest quality. (B) This means your production line will not be shut down, due to poor-quality Doogers, and your profits will be maximized. (C) Increased profit is our goal, don't you agree?"

I'm going to suggest that you _never_ introduce a product or service feature without converting it to a customer benefit and gaining a commitment regarding its value from the customer. Obviously, if the customer does not agree that our feature will benefit him, let's talk about something else. If he doesn't like _that_ advantage, how about _this_ advantage?

Please pause right now and write down ways in which you might phrase Advantages and Benefits and request Commitments for _your_ product or service.

A _____
 _____

B _____
 _____

C _____
 _____

A _____
  _____
B _____
  _____
C _____
  _____

A _____
  _____
B _____
  _____
C _____
  _____

A _____
  _____
B _____
  _____
C _____
  _____

A _____
  _____
B _____
  _____
C _____
  _____

The point of the A.B.C. demonstration is to bring the customer to the realization of a *Bottom line:* a benefit the customer does not now have and cannot obtain elsewhere. When, and *only* when, we can provide a bottom line valuable to our customer, his decision will be relatively easy. Objections will be less important, problems less formidable, and price differentials minimized. Clearly, if we have something of value to the customer that he cannot get from anyone else, our price becomes relatively unimportant. The more he wants it, the less important price becomes. Ever price a heart transplant? Those things cost a bundle. Yet I have it on good authority that heart surgeons seldom negotiate fees. They are dealing with *motivated* buyers.

A great bottom line will give you a decided advantage over your competition. Several great bottom lines will make you nearly invincible.

Please pause for a few minutes and, using the A.B.C. approach, jot down at least five *bottom lines* for your product or service.

1. A. _____
   B. _____
   C. _____

2. A. _____
   B. _____
   C. _____

3. A. _____
   B. _____
   C. _____

4. A. _____

   B. _____

   C. _____

5. A. _____

   B. _____

   C. _____

13
THE MOMENT OF TRUTH

"The race is not always to the swift, nor the battle to the strong, but that's the way to bet."

—Damon Runyon

Now we have accurately divined the customer's needs and demonstrated how our product will solve his problems. It's on toward time to close. After all, if it's worth doing, it's worth doing for money.

Assuming that we've done our job correctly to this point, the close should flow in as a natural and comfortable part of our presentation. Yet in the real world, it seldom seems to. Research indicates that *63 percent of all sales presentations end without the salesperson having asked for the order.*

Ain't that the *pits?* Now, I'm not really a big baseball fan. I think it's kind of a dull game. But can you imagine how dull baseball would be if, out of every 100 batters who came to the plate, only 37 bothered to swing at the ball?

How can we hope to close sales if we don't ask people to buy?

A number of years ago, a friend of mine, Art Godi, suggested that possibly we were confusing our new salespeople with too much information. That we might be more effective if we simply had them ask people, "Would you like to own this home?" each time they showed a property. It sounded good to me, so we started teaching it in our company training program.

We were representing a builder in the sale of some relatively expensive homes called "The Woodlands." Our experienced salespeople didn't like to sit in model homes, so we put our "green peas" out there. They called it "the leper colony." A couple came by, and were met by one of our bright young stars, Terry Davis. He showed them through the models, gave them a brochure, and watched them walking to the parking lot. Only then did it strike him that he had forgotten to ask them to buy. It was a warm day, so they were sitting in their car with the windows up and the engine and air conditioning running, studying the brochure, when Terry came up to knock on their window. You see, he was too new new and green to know you simply don't do that sort of thing. When the woman rolled down her window, Terry said, "I forgot to ask you, and my broker says always to ask . . . would you like to own one of those homes?" The husband was stunned. He looked blankly at his wife, who was nodding rapidly. He turned to Terry and said, "Yeah, I guess we would." They turned off the engine, went to the sales office, and bought one.

Terry sold his first home because he didn't know it was dumb to ask everyone to buy. Unfortunately, as he gained experience, he learned to be more worldly and sophisticated. He's no longer in selling. Philosopher William Feather wrote, "Experience and enthusiasm are two fine business attributes, seldom found in one individual."

The single greatest mistake made by salespeople today is to not ask for the order. And even those who do ask, quit too soon. Of those salespeople who ask for the order at all,

44% quit after one "no"
22% quit after two "no's"
14% quit after three "no's"
12% quit after four "no's"

This totals 92 percent. This means that after four "no's," 92 percent of your competition is out in the parking lot, all four feet sticking straight up in the air. For years we have been told that 80 percent of the business is done by 20 percent of the salespeople, but let's consider this: *Sixty percent of all buyers say "no" four times before they say "yes."* If 92 percent of our competition is out of the running after four "no's," this must mean that 8 percent of the salespeople get 60 percent of the business, *just by asking.*

Here's the real key to selling: *You ask, you get.* The more you ask, the more you get. If you don't ask, you don't get. You can go to all the seminars that come to your town, read all the books, listen to all the tapes. If you don't learn to ask, you're going to go broke.

I once worked with a man named Ralph Cooley. He was the most offensive human being I have ever known. He had store teeth. You knew that, as he kept them in his coat pocket. He always needed a shave. In his other coat pocket he carried a bottle half full of warm coke, half full of Bourbon. He seldom made any sense after noon. His breath was like an acetylene torch. He never went to seminars, never bought a book, and hated sales meetings. But, Ralph was always in the top three because he was a terrific asker. You'd either buy from Ralph or want to hit him.

Obviously, if we take advantage of all the education available to us *and* learn to ask, we'll be invincible.

I believe one reason we fail to consistently ask for the order is that we don't clearly know *when* to ask. In my first sales seminar, J. Douglas Edwards said, "The only way you'll ever learn when to close is by closing too early, too often, and too hard." *Bull*. I'm here to guarantee you that if you close people too often, too early, and too hard, they will make rude remarks about your parents.

When salespeople close too early, too often, and too hard, the only thing they learn is not to close at all—because closing hurts. Mark Twain wrote, "If a cat sits on a hot stove, he'll never sit on a hot stove again. But, for that matter, he'll never sit on a cold stove either. . . . He's flat out of the business of sitting on stoves." If, every time we close, we are rejected, we soon learn that closing is not what you'd call fun. And we're flat out of the business of closing.

In every successful sale, there is a *magic moment*, when the buyer will be most likely to sign the order. Close too soon, and we may get an objection or stall. Close too late and we'll almost always talk our way right out of the sale. Far more sales are lost by talking past the magic moment than by closing too soon.

How then, you might well inquire, do we detect this magic moment? By the age-old process of elimination. Our customers can hold only one of three attitudes at any time. These attitudes are:

Objection
Indifference
Acceptance

The very basis of simplified selling is the realization that our customers can possess *only* these three attitudes and can hold *only one* of these attitudes at any given time. Some ambivalence can exist, true. But it is clearly impossible for a customer to be in definite states of acceptance and objection at the same time. If we can accurately determine the customer's attitude and know how to appropriately respond to that attitude, the business of selling gets simple.

Let's look at each of these attitudes, determine how we might recognize them, and develop appropriate responses.

OBJECTION

When the customer voices direct opposition to our proposal, or a portion of it, he might say something like "Your price is too high," or "Your delivery is slow," or "That color is terrible."

Those new to selling are often terrified by objections, but there is really nothing to fear. Objections don't get in the way of the sales process; they are a *part* of the sales process. An objection often indicates a sincere interest in the proposal on the part of the customer.

The old line on selling dictated that we should devote a great deal of our learning time to overcoming objections. That true selling began *only* when an objection arose. That objections were the call to arms, the sounding of the battle clarion. "Grab your book of prepared responses and *go crush those objections.*"

Bull. An objection merely means that the customer is sharing with us a problem, as he sees it. Actually, as we do a better job in the first initial steps of our sales process, the number of objections we encounter will markedly decrease. After all, if we clearly understand the customer's problems and have shown him a good method of solving those problems, what's to object to? Nevertheless, in the very best of sales presentations, objections do come up and must be dealt with.

Probably the most frequently encountered error in dealing with objections is to give them too much weight and to jump on them too fast. In buying the Mercedes-Benz, I had said, "They sure cost a lot of money." That could be construed as an objection, and by most salespeople, would be. The average salesperson would immediately begin to demonstrate how wrong I was, and how the Mercedes-Benz was easily worth every dime being asked for it. By so doing, he would have put me in a defensive position. I would have had to defend why I was right and why the car was, in fact, extremely expensive. The more I said about the car costing a lot of money, the more I would have sold myself on that point of view. Not this dealer. He was way too smart for that. He simply acknowledged my point of view by saying, "Yeah, they *do* cost a lot of money, don't they?" He withheld support, either positive or negative, from me. He left me out there all alone with a neutral, nonthreatening statement. He showed that he understood my point of view, but did not argue with it.

The first time you hear an objection, *ignore it*. That's right, withhold support, either positive or negative, and the majority of the objections you encounter will simply go away and never arise again.

> CUSTOMER: "Your price is too high."
> US: "I understand."
> CUSTOMER: "Your delivery is too slow."
> US: "Uh huh."
> CUSTOMER: "That color is horrible."
> US: (Silence)

This approach is kind of hard to get used to, but try it. You'll be amazed. In the absence of support from us, most objections simply go away. Trust me, if the objection is really important to the customer, he'll bring it up again. He might say something like, "What do you mean 'I understand'? Your damn price is too high." Terrific. Now we have an objection important to the customer and we can deal with it. Only when it comes up twice is an objection sufficiently serious to merit our concern.

Let's look at one step-by-step method for dealing with objections, related in this case to price. Price is one of the more frequently encountered objections, as few of us have the least costly product or service in our field. That's good, because if we are always the lowest-priced, that means we can't be making enough profit. Robert Ringer summed it up: "Closing deals is so much trash, if you, my friend, don't get no *cash*." If you never encounter a price objection, seriously consider changing your line, or raising your price. You're leaving money on the table.

The way to deal with objections is to *flow with them*. Assume that a customer says: "I'm afraid your price is just too high."

Step 1: *Be happy*. I did not say "act happy"; that would be hypocritical. Rather, *be* happy. We can be sincerely happy, as the objection is one we can deal with. Our happiness might be evidenced by a statement such as: "That's an interesting point [not a problem, not an objection] you bring up and I'm delighted that you did. Now we can discuss it." Isn't that a non-abrasive statement? This is the age of non-adversary selling. This person is not our enemy, so we'll flow with him, minimizing resistance.

One of the primary rules for getting feedback is to *reward* it when you get it. There may be some feedback you'd rather not hear, but there's no such thing as bad feedback.

We may not be too thrilled to hear an objection, but at least we know what it is and can try to deal with it. If we don't reward the feedback, we'll stop getting it and will be operating in the dark.

Step 2: *Rephrase in question form.* When I was much younger, on occasion I'd do a magnificent job of overcoming—in fact, crushing—an objection, only to find that it was the wrong objection. That wasn't what the customer meant at all. We must rephrase the objection until we state the customer's feelings to his complete satisfaction. As long as he says, "No, that's not quite it," it isn't. We simply can't proceed until we and the customer are in complete agreement as to the exact nature of the problem. It might go something like this:

> CUSTOMER: "Your price is too high."
> US: "Are you saying it's more than you can afford to pay?" [Note: this question has historically been used as a manipulation to induce guilt on the part of the customer. This is not the intent here. There's a big difference between what we can afford to pay and what we will pay, sometimes. I want to know where the customer is coming from.]
> CUSTOMER: "I didn't say that. I can afford it, I just don't want to pay that amount."
> US: "Have you seen other products that fill your needs for less money?"
> CUSTOMER: "Well, Fezler's Frammis seems to do about the same thing, and their price is a little lower."

Aha, now we're getting to the central issue. We have a little competition. This is no biggie, though; we're used to competition.

Step 3: *Isolate the objection.*

US: "Besides price, is there anything else that would prevent us from going ahead now?"

Here, the objective is to find out if there's anything else that's troubling the customer. If so, maybe we're running down the wrong road, hopelessly lost but making excellent time. It's really easy to get into a game we cannot win of seeing if we can knock down objections faster than the customer can think them up.

Here's the ultimate heresy, according to the old line. Sometimes it may not be in the customer's best interest to buy our stuff. If we are in agreement that our job is simply to help customers make good decisions, then we must be aware that we won't sell them all. If the customer is simply trying to think up objections so as to make us go away, why not save everybody's time and just leave?

Now, I'm not advocating packing up at the first sign of resistance. I *am* saying that if the relationship has deteriorated to the point where the customer is trying to dream up ways to get rid of me, I'm going to do my part. For situations like these, I love this approach: "When I came in here, you only had one problem. Now you have two. The second one is how to get rid of me, and that's easy. Tell me and I'll go. As long as I'm here, however, doesn't it make sense for us to work on the first problem?" This sort of direct bluntness will often pop the true problem out of the customer. At worst he'll know we're not to be trifled with, and we'll feel good. Occasionally it's just good business to let an obstinate, cantankerous customer see the mistletoe on your coattail.

Assume the customer is not evil and says, "No. Price is the only problem. If you match Fezler's Frammis, you've got a deal." We're on to the next step.

Step 4: *Deal with it.* Objections come in two general

151

categories: easy ones and hard ones. Let's do easy ones first, as they're easier. *Deal with easy objections head-on.* Some objections are so easy that we fantasize about their coming up. As an example, we just heard that Fezler went broke last week, due to price-slashing, and will no longer be around to bug us. The great temptation is to share this information at the first mention of Fezler, but it can be far more powerful if saved until the first three steps are completed. Then there's no way we're not going to get an order.

Most often price, in general, is an easy objection. The importance of price is in inverse proportion to the desire of the customer. Succinctly stated, the only time price is important is when they don't want it badly enough.

One method of dealing with a price problem is to reduce it to reality. This can be done when the price will be paid in payments, the benefit of the product will be spread over a number of people, or the price is divisible by any mathematical unit.

Let's examine a differential in price when the product will be paid for in installments. We and the customer are in agreement that our Fairdinkum Frammis will suit his needs better than Fezler's Frammis. We could write the order today were it not for a $1,000 price differential between us and that rotten Fezler. We have further determined that the purchase will be financed over a 36-month period at about a 20 percent annual percentage rate. We consult our handy-dandy rate chart and find that $1,000 over 36 months at 20 percent will pay off at $37.16 per month. Our conversation might run along these lines.

> US: "As I see it, we've got about a $1,000 total difference. Is that about it?"
> CUSTOMER: "Yup."
> US: "Write this down, please."

Let me here interject a personal perception. I believe the use of pocket calculators has done more to hinder communication between buyers and sellers than any other single device. We punch buttons, lights flash, and numbers appear magically. Nobody knows how it happened. Leprechauns must live in there. I believe people do not trust that which they don't understand. When figuring in a sales situation, always let the customer work the pencil. Anything he writes down, he'll believe. It's *his* number. Secondly, customers won't write down anything they don't understand. They'll therefore never have the feeling you've tricked them.

Now assume the customer has taken down the figures.

> US: "The chart here shows a payment of $37 and change on a $1,000 loan. Do you imagine, in the average month, you'd use your Frammis about 30 days?"
> CUSTOMER: "I guess so."
> US: "Would you please divide the $37 by 30 days?"
> CUSTOMER: "Let's see, 37 divided by 30 is $1.23."
> US: "Are you saying that $1.23 a day is going to be the difference between what you really want and what you feel you have to settle for?"

Let's face it, sport fans, most of our customers will *spill* that much each day, if they drink at all. This approach used to be called "reducing to the ridiculous," but I don't see it that way. People buy on dollars down and dollars per month. I see it as our responsibility to talk with them in terms to which they can relate.

Hard objections are aptly named. Sometimes customers are going to bring up problems for which you have no good answers. I won't bother to elucidate; you know very well what I mean. They're just *hard*.

When someone gives us a hard objection, we must introduce additional benefits of ownership that will help us neutralize the objection. We just fall back a step, and using the A.B.C. formula, introduce additional benefits.

When faced with objections, easy or hard, one of our finest allies is the *proof source book*. Many salespeople use presentation manuals, or pitch books, which outline, in nauseating detail, the virtues of the salesperson and his or her company. My experience with these is that they induce slumber on the part of the customer faster than Nitol. Again, people buy for their reasons, not ours. A pitch book can only contain *our* reasons for why they should buy.

A proof source book, on the other hand, allows us to offer proof of any statement the customer might doubt. A simple scrapbook with graphs, articles, pictures, and reference letters is usually sufficient.

If someone says your Belchfire 4 is priced too high, you are then in a position to prove that the Sloshpot 6 is even higher-priced by the time you add on all the equipment that comes standard on the Belchfire.

When someone evidences concern about the reliability of your Sentence Master, you can furnish letters of praise from satisfied customers.

When a customer is afraid she might be paying too much for a home, you can show her what other homes in the area have sold for and show her the annual average rate of appreciation in your area.

A proof source book helps us provide factual justification for the emotional decisions our customers make. If maintaining optimum credibility is your objective, *never* say anything you can't prove. When you make a flat statement, which is challenged, and you can't prove what you said, your credibility goes right down the pipe.

Conversely, never prove anything the customer already believes. We spend a lot of time and effort gathering and assembling proof sources. The tendency is to try to recoup that effort by showing the book to anyone who will remain stationary long enough. There are two problems with this:

1. Many people don't give a damn and will be bored to tears.

2. When you set out to prove something that the customer already believes, you nonverbally communicate that maybe it really isn't true, or you wouldn't go to such great lengths to try to prove it. In either event, your credibility suffers.

Clearly, the best way to handle objections is to do such a thorough job of customer diagnosis and product demonstration that we eliminate the objections before we even get this far. It's a lot easier to stomp on little snakes than to let them grow up big and bite you.

INDIFFERENCE

Indifference is indicated by customers' statements such as: "I want to think it over," or "My old car still runs all right," or "I'll sell my home myself and save the commission," or "I'm in no real hurry."

The customer is saying, in effect, that he is really not sold yet. He is not sufficiently uncomfortable with his present situation, or is not convinced that your proposal will help it any.

Such indifference often stems from the basic four "no's" of selling:

- *No trust.* I really don't fully trust you.
- *No need.* I'm not aware of a need for your product or service.
- *No help.* I'm aware of a need, but am not sold on the idea that your product or service will satisfy it.
- *No hurry.* O.K., you can satisfy my need, but my problem doesn't really bother me enough yet for me to pay to make it go away.

Usually, when the four "no's" have been recognized and dealt with, a sale is made. When we perceive that the customer's attitude is one of indifference, we probe. We probe for areas of discomfort or areas of dissatisfaction with his present status. In responding to our probes, the customer will often discover the problem and the solution without our having to point them out. We are nearly always more comfortable with things we discover ourselves.

You'll recall we discussed the fine art of probing in Chapter 2. Nondirective probes are terrific for getting information for us. However, directive probes are more effective for elevating the consciousness of the customer. We use a directive probe to draw the customer's attention to areas of need we think should be addressed, or areas of discomfort the customer may have overlooked:

Some examples:

"Is there something specifically concerning you?"
"What kind of gas mileage is your old car giving you?"
"Had any major repair bills lately?"
"Are you having much luck attracting customers for your home?"

"What would your assistants be able to do for you if they had more time?"

"If we could save you X dollars per week, starting next week, would you still rather wait six months?"

Let's pause a few minutes and have you write down ten directive probes that can be applied to the indifference you encounter in your field.

1. _____

2. _____

3. _____

4. _____

5. _____

6. _____

7. _____

8. _____

9. _____

10. _____

ACCEPTANCE

When we perceive the customer's attitude is one of acceptance, we *close*. You bend the horseshoe when it's hot. No more conversation, just go for it. The magic moment is usually a very narrow window and is readily overshot. I've seen countless salespeople spend half an hour selling their program and two hours buying it back. When the light goes on, *close*.

Do we really need 75 closes? Of course not. All we need is one, if it makes good sense and *if we use it.*

The old standby summary close is effective and fits right in with the open, honest, intimate relationship we've tried to build from the opening word. We simply summarize those benefits *important to the customer* and request action.

If I haven't already sold you on the need for taking notes, let me try again. If, in the earlier stages of the sale, we have not written down those benefits important to the customer, we'll forget them. When we forget what's important to the customer, we, being human, will talk to the customer about that which is important to us and therefore *should* be important to the customer. Since people buy for their reasons, not ours, it's critical that we summarize only those benefits important to them.

What, specifically, do we say? Anything you want to say, obviously. I usually say something along this line when I sense the customer's attitude is one of acceptance:

"Let's review the things you have told me were important to you. You indicated high quality was paramount, and it's been proved that our product has the highest acceptance rates in the industry. You want prompt delivery and we have demonstrated 97 percent on-time delivery. You wanted a competitive price and we have it. It looks as if all we need to get started is your signature. Press hard, the fourth copy's yours."

But, you might ask, what will happen to us if we've misjudged the customer's attitude? What if it really wasn't acceptance? What if we've missed the magic moment? No problem. If we're wrong, and we often are, the customer will tell us. Remember, there are only three possible attitudes the customer can have, and he can only hold one of those attitudes at any given time. If indeed the customer's attitude is acceptance, he'll probably sign. If the attitude is objection, he'll object—and that's O.K. We know how to flow with objections. If his attitude is indifference, he'll probably stall or want to "think it over"; that's O.K., too. We know that when the customer's attitude is one of indifference, we probe for areas of discomfort or areas of need.

The basic fact is this: We have developed the flexibility to flow with the customer wherever he goes. This eliminates the need for pressure, manipulation, and the attendant stress. Selling is comfortable and fun again.

Whenever you're in doubt as to the attitude of the customer, try a close. You have absolutely nothing to lose.

14
WRITE WHEN YOU GET WORK

*"The World is full of willing people: some willing
to work, the rest willing to let them."*

—Robert Frost

So now the fish is in the boat and we're ready to go out
and look for the next one, right? *Wrong.* Now is our opportunity to clearly distinguish ourselves from the mob.
Truly excellent salespeople do things that ordinary salespeople are unwilling, or unable, to do. A sampling of responses from a great number of customers for a wide range
of products and services has shown that the most common
complaint is being dropped like a hot rock as soon as the
order is signed.

A short "thank you" note takes but seconds to write, but
will help embed you fondly in the memory of your customer
forever. Think about it. When was the last time you received a note, thanking you for your business, from a person
from whom you bought something? No, I don't mean a

computer-printed form letter from the company. I mean an honest-to-God handwritten note from a real person. If you've *ever* received one, you have dealt with an unusual salesperson. Did it make you feel good? You bet, and we can generate that same warm feeling in our customers for the price of postage and a very few minutes. Drop them each a short note and let them know how much you appreciate their contribution to your net worth.

For those of us who have interest in *really* cementing a relationship, a small gift is certainly in order. I don't mean a lavish outpouring of funds but a small, thoughtful gift. A little remembrance of you. Possibly a set of floor mats for a new car. Or a couple of extra print wheels for the new word processor. Or a hand-knitted diode warmer for the new Dooger. No commercial message. No request for referrals. Just a gift because you enjoyed doing business with them. When people enjoy buying from you, they want their friends to share the pleasure, and referrals just flow in.

Let's remember the last time we made a major purchase. The first 72 hours after delivery are the toughest, aren't they? We are excited about our purchase and boring our acquaintances with stories of our negotiating prowess. At the same time, we suffer some insecurities. Maybe we paid too much. Maybe we should have shopped more. Maybe it'll break. The damn thing doesn't seem to work quite the way we thought it would. During the first 72 hours of ownership we're as excited about our purchase as we'll ever be. We also have fears that will gradually begin to diminish. It is during these first 72 hours of ownership that a call from the salesperson is most needed and appreciated. It will be most effective in lending support and alleviating the dread "buyer's remorse." Calls made during this period will also be most likely to yield the names of other prospective purchasers.

162

Here's the problem with making follow-up calls. Sometimes you'll get heat. The customer is emotionally involved and has encountered a problem with his new purchase. This problem has magnified in his mind to the point where all else is eclipsed. Then you call. You immediately become the great receptacle for bile and hatred. This part of the job is not tremendous fun, but it goes with the territory.

Now is the time for patient listening, empathy, support, and *action*. The customer has a problem, so *we* have a problem. Let's get about solving it—*now!*

Those of you who were with us in Chapter 9 will be delighted to know I finally bought a word processor. Oh, I'm still writing with a pencil, as I can't run the damn thing, but at least I now own a word processor.

What happened was, I met a very well-groomed, pleasant, enthusiastic young woman named Mary Lou Crall. She knows quite a bit about word processing and a whole lot about people. She found out what I wanted the beast to do and showed me how her machine would do it. She used nice terms like "user friendly." She convinced me that the thing was so simple, even I could operate it—the only area in which she strayed from the truth. In less than two hours, she had me on an order for a word processor costing $4,000 more than I had planned to spend. I was *ecstatic*.

Then the phone calls from other salespeople and even some of my friends began to come in. "You bought a *what?*" "You paid *how much?*" "How long is the warranty?" Hell, I don't know. "Will it do automatic pagination?" What's automatic pagination? "How many w.p.m. will the printer do?" I don't remember. "How many bytes of storage in the random access memory?" I think I'm going to be sick. I get *so* depressed.

Then a letter from Mary Lou came, assuring me that I had contracted for the most advanced and reliable piece of electronic intellect ever to enlighten the life of modern man. I felt a little better. The nausea began to subside.

The next day Mary Lou called to reassure me again and confirm the delivery date. I asked her all the hard questions that had been asked of me. She answered every one and let me know that no finer electronic servant was available at *any* price, much less the pittance I had paid. I was *so* excited. I could hardly wait for delivery.

The great day dawned, and that leering, humming one-eyed monster was firmly ensconced in my office, which we had to totally rearrange to accommodate it. (Moving furniture is not my long suit.) It took less than two hours for that machine to elevate my office manager and me to the level of conscious incompetence. We couldn't drive the beast. We couldn't even get it to *type*. During a momentary power outage, it became cannibalistic and *ate* its own memory bank. In my entire life I have never experienced such hatred, fear of, and loathing for an inanimate object.

Mary Lou called. "How's the new baby?" she said. I shared my discomfort with her. I even seem to recall saying something about putting it "where the sun doesn't shine." I was totally irrational and a good deal less than kind.

She remained calm. She listened to my depraved ranting and periodically summed up my threats to let me know she clearly understood the problem. When my screaming subsided to muffled sobs, she said she'd be right out to show us which buttons to push. Acting on risk of life and limb, she was *right out*. She pushed buttons. Lights blinked, motors whirred, and typewritten sheets spewed forth with amazing ease. She calmly pointed out that when my secretary Carolyn had received the necessary training, she too would be able to litter the floor with typewritten pages.

She showed me again the fantastic capabilities of our electronic friend.

I *love* my word processor. I can't drive it, but I love it. I gave Mary Lou a referral and doubtless will give her many more. She's wonderful.

Mary Lou had no control over the events that transpired, but she did manage to affect the way I *felt* about the events that transpired. Most importantly, she was *there*. Had she not made those calls, I probably wouldn't still own my wonderful word processor today. And I'd be poorer for the loss.

Our follow-up, concern, and presence are probably the most essential part of building our business for tomorrow.

15
KEEPING THE WHEELS ON

*"Instead of loving your enemies, treat your
friends a little better."*

—*Ed Howe*

The career you and I have chosen to pursue has one of the
highest rates of turnover known to modern man. Most people drop out of selling within the first six months. They
never learn to sell. They can't make enough to live on, and
are just blown out of the water. I'm not concerned about
them. That's just the way it goes in a business with the
ease of entry ours has.

I'm concerned about *you*. People who may find themselves in the sophomore slump. You see, the second greatest point of egress from the selling field is two to three
years out. You've learned how to sell. You're making a
decent living, but the business isn't fun any more. People
call you at all hours of the day and night and tell you what
they're going to do to you. You're working too hard. Your

kids call you "sir" (and spell it "cur"). Your days all seem pretty much the same. You're going nowhere fast, on the treadmill to salespeople's oblivion.

Sound vaguely familiar? If you've been in selling for more than twenty minutes, you know that all your days in selling are not going to be good ones. We need effective means for getting through the bad days, so we can really *live* through the good ones. If you can't feel really good about yourself and your business, I defy you to do a good job of selling, or anything else for that matter. You must keep yourself bright and shiny, for you are the window through which you see the world.

There have been many fine books written on how to deal with stress, and I commend them to you. I believe, however, that the finest tool for stress relief is a warm and loving home. We all need a safe harbor. A place where they can't get at us. A place where you can just be you—wander around in your shorts and scratch wherever it itches (you hadn't ought to do that in the office).

And yet, being human, we all tend to foul up that which is most important to us by bringing our bad days home with us to share. We walk in the house and promptly dump our bucket on the family.

Tonight, in your town, Seymour Seller will rush to the side of his lovely wife Serene and the first words out of his mouth will be, "Boy, did I have a bitch of a day. That deal I've been working on for thirteen months—it's been a heavy one. Well, he bought today. But from the competition. I had a career adjustment meeting with the boss. He said I've got thirty days to get some marks on the board or he can no longer afford the luxury of my association. I told you about the Frumps—Farley and Felicia Frump—the ones with the two little daughters in sailor suits? Well, they were in again today. One of those kids threw up all over my desk. I'm so depressed. Get me a bottle of Ripple with a nipple on it. I'm going to my room."

Now what's Serene Seller going to say? "Poor baby?" Not on your life. She's going to say, "You think *you* had a bitch of a day. Wait'll you hear about mine. Your banker's now calling *me* about your note. He says you've got five days to cover it, or he'll put the hook on your car. Speaking of cars, mine's making that funny little noise again. If you had a *real* job, you could get me a new one, like Alice has. The school called about little Harvey, your pride and joy, your only son. He's been wearing makeup again."

Now how warm and loving is your safe harbor? You can't have a safe harbor if you just run in and dump all your problems on your spouse. The poor dear, just standing there waiting to greet you, and out of the blue she gets hit with a full bucket. Mind you, I'm not suggesting that you not dump your bucket. You can't go all through life with a full bucket. Can you imagine how long your arms would get? What you can do, however, is give enough positive input so that your spouse can stand your dumping a little of the bucket. We all know that when we have had lots of positives and feel good, a little negativity does no harm.

I'm going to suggest something that may seem weird and patently perverted to you. I'm going to suggest you resume cuddling. Remember how much fun that was *before* you got married? Could hardly wait to get your hands on her, right? Then you got licensed. Now, if your wife is silly enough to want to throw her arms around you, you bellow, "What the hell you doing? I just got this suit out of the cleaners. You'll wrinkle it all up. Sex maniac. Don't you ever think about anything else? What's for dinner?" It doesn't take but about thirty days to cure a person of the filthy habit. Now she wouldn't touch you with a stick.

Go back to cuddling. Cuddling is one of the most intense

strokes one person can give another, aside from sex, which is inconvenient in public (oh, I know it's *done*). When you go home, before you say anything, just grab hold and cuddle for a couple of minutes. (Note: If you've been married more than a year, be sure to tell your wife what you're doing or she'll want to know where you've been all afternoon, minute by minute.) Before you doze off at night, cuddle for a couple of minutes. Now I know you went to a meeting on positive thinking and they told you to jump up every morning, breathe deeply, holler "Good morning, God," and dive into a brisk cold shower. *Bull.* Stay in bed and cuddle for a couple of minutes—that's a lot more fun. So you occasionally miss a sales meeting, so what? There'll be another one next week. Again, before you leave the house, grab hold and cuddle for a couple of minutes. Lots of cuddling goes a long way toward solidifying your feelings toward your spouse and creating a safe harbor.

After you've cuddled and before you dump your bucket, tell your spouse three positive things.

1. *Something nice about him or her.* Is this always easy? God, no. Sometimes you really have to dig for it. "Darling, those are probably the nicest rollers I've ever seen in your hair. The way you've color-coordinated them with that chenille robe is really terrific. That much metal up there, I'll bet you draw a good, clear picture."

2. *The* best *thing that's happened to you today.* Is this always easy? Not a bit easier than number 1. "The most wonderful thing happened today. I told you about the Frumps? Farley and Felicia and the two little daughters in sailor suits? Well, they were in today and it was wonderful. One of those kids threw up all over my desk and *didn't get any on me*. She aimed at me all right, but I

dodged—and *look*, my clothes are cleaner than a hound's tooth.

3. *The most important thing you've learned and how you're going to use it to improve your business or your life.* You must have learned something during the last twenty-four-hour period. Share this knowledge with your spouse.

A safe harbor needs to be just that: a place of respite from daily business pressures, a place where you can go and let your eyeballs sink back in. Most people cannot be creative while under pressure, yet some folks take their work home with them. There's something so odd going on in California that you're going to find it hard to believe— at least, I did. If it ever happens in your town, it'll do more to run you out of selling than anything else I know. Now I know my telling you this will damage my credibility, as it's so hard to believe, but please trust me, it's actually happening. Some people in real estate, in California, are *putting their home phone numbers on their business cards.* There, I knew you'd find it hard to believe. I've asked them, "Why do you do that?" They say, "I must be responsive to my customers. If they can't reach me, I might miss a deal."

Let me give you the alternative. You might miss your life. There is a lot more to life than selling stuff, and it goes by *so* fast. You might wake up one morning, nearly fifty, having raised three kids, and find out you'd missed the whole thing. The other day I said to my lovely wife, "Barbara, didn't we used to have kids around here?" She said, "Yeah, but they all grew up and left." I said, "Damn, I missed it. Must have been at the office."

You see, I can tell you accurately about all these cowpies on the selling road, as I've stepped in every one of them. I will even admit that I used to have my home phone number on my business card. My business card was a thing of wonder. In fact, are you ready to be impressed? Every year, at its convention, the National Association of Realtors holds a contest honoring, among other things, business cards and letterheads. In 1973, I won first place for business cards and letterhead in the United States of America. There, I knew you'd be impressed. But in this case it was kind of like getting your face on the cover of *Sports Illustrated*: it means you're about to go into a slump. In 1973 I won the contest; in 1975 I lost the company. It was my most memorable ego enema.

My business card was a thing of beauty to behold. Under a fold-over flap it had my office phone number. (I went to a seminar where they told me that was a good idea.) It had a private office number so people could circumvent the receptionist and surprise me. They did. It had my home phone number. I told people to call me anytime. They did. It had my car phone number. If you want a thrill, try driving down a six-lane elevated California freeway at 85 miles per hour and having your phone go off. You change six lanes so fast, you'll not even know you did it. Only my laundry and I knew how that upset me. The last number was one they could call twenty-four hours a day, and one of those devilish beepers would go off in my pocket. This always scared me half to death, as I knew the odds were overwhelming that the news was *bad*. Nobody ever tries that hard to find you to give you good news.

I went on this way for over seven years. I don't want to tell you I was nervous, but I was incredibly alert. People called me at all hours, telling me what they were going to do to me as soon as I came into the office. Is it any wonder I had trouble getting to the office on time in the morning? If you know your office is full of alligators, just waiting for you, there's little joy in getting there on time.

I'm further going to suggest it's not even good business to take business calls at home, if you're doing what you should be doing at home—relaxing and letting your warts show. A number of years ago, a friend of mine was visiting my home for dinner. Now I don't really like gin, but my friend does and I'm a gracious host, so I mixed us up martinis in mason jars. We had one and he uttered words that should be inscribed in granite somewhere. He said, "Martinis are just like breasts. One's not enough and three's too many." We had three. Then it was dinnertime. Of course you realize that, in California, wine isn't considered booze; it's food, and I want my guests to be well fed. I had an old bottle of Cabernet Sauvignon that I'd been saving for a special occasion, and this was clearly it. I pulled the cork, poured him one glass, and drank the rest.

About 9:30, one of my best customers called me. Why? Because I had *told* him to call me anytime he had a question. I answered the telephone exhibiting my best professional demeanor, by saying, "Hullo. Thish is Hank Trishler." Being an obliging sort of a person, he called me at my office the next morning. He said, "I hope you're feeling better. You didn't sound so hot when I talked with you last night." I said, "Last night?" I didn't even remember he had called.

I cannot believe that my conduct that evening did anything to elevate his opinion of my professional ability. How would you like to call up your brain surgeon and find he's juiced out of his gourd? The choice then became crystal clear to me. Either I had to get a safe harbor where I could just be me, with dimples and warts, *or* I had to give up booze. There was no contest.

Now I don't want to tell you I immediately took all my numbers off my cards. No, I had bought into the line of thought about giving home numbers, and was afraid it would cost me money. I wanted to try to find out how much it would cost me, so I bought 100 business cards with only my office number on them and shuffled them in with my sharpshooter cards. Then, when I'd give out a card, I'd watch carefully to see how many people were offended by not receiving my home number. *Not one.* Conversely, not one person who *did* receive my home number said, "Oh great, your home number. Of course I'll do business with you. I've been dying to do business with someone at his home." The fact of the matter is, *nobody cared.* Guess what? People stopped calling me at home, and now I go into the office expecting to find alligators lying in wait for me, but at least I didn't have to know about them beforehand.

> People treat us the way we have *trained* them to treat us.

If you don't like the way people are treating you, just change the training.

If we're not going to do business at home, we'd better do some someplace, or we're going to go broke. Six hours a day, five days a week is plenty, provided that we really *work* during those hours. If you're not taking business calls at home, does it make sense to take personal calls at work? Not hardly. The concept here is:

> Wherever you are, be there.

Somewhere today, there's a guy sitting in his office, thinking about taking his son fishing. There's also a guy on a lake, fishing with his son and thinking about business. Neither one of them is anywhere. When you go to work, *work.* When your calls are made, *go home*—all of you. Wherever you are, be there.

When I do real estate seminars, an odd thing happens— more so at real estate programs than at any other sales programs I do. Every time we have a break, or a lunch period, the pay phones load up with people calling their offices to get bad news. I used to do that, too. A few years ago I was attending a one-day seminar for which I had paid

$295. It's amazing, when you spend $295 for a seminar, what good notes you take. By noon, I had seven legal-length pages, single-spaced on both sides. I had white, cramped fingers from writing so much. It was great and I was excited.

At noon, I called my office. Why? I dunno. It was like a subconscious message from God: "Call your office." So I did. My secretary recognized me right off; she's good.

She said, "Hank. Thank heaven you called." I've learned to hate conversations that begin that way.

I said, "Is there a problem?"

She said, "Is there a *problem*? It's Bob Walker, and he's madder than a mashed cat."

I said, "What's he mad about?"

She said, "I don't know, but he said if you don't call him right back, it's going in the dumper."

I said, "*What's* going in the dumper?"

She said, "I don't know. He hung up."

Now if you've been in selling for more than a month, you've probably received such a call. If you have received such a call, you're also familiar with the natural law which states that a salesperson will never go to a pay phone with more than one dime. I had to lose my position in the phone line, go to the gift shop, and get another dime. I asked the folks in line at the phone if they'd let me have my place back. They said "no," so I had to wait while three other people got dumped on by their offices.

I called Bob Walker. Cynthia, his secretary said, "Hank. Thank heaven you called."

I said, "I'm hearing that a lot this morning. Is there a problem?"

She said, "Is there a *problem*! It's Bob. He's incoherent with rage."

I said, "What's he mad about?"

She said, "I don't know. He's so mad, he won't even talk to me. All he's done all morning is slam drawers and bang doors and scream 'I'm going to get that son of a bitch.'"

She had my attention. I said, "Well, let me talk to him. I'm sure we'll straighten it out."

She said, "I can't. He's on the other line, talking to his attorney."

I was concerned. I said, "Put me on hold and get me in as soon as he hangs up."

She said, "I will." Then she cut me off.

I had to get out of line and get another dime. This time I only had to wait while two people got dumped on by their offices. My palms were sweating profusely. I finally got Cynthia and shrieked, "You cut me off!"

She blubbered, "I'm sorry, Hank, I was so nervous, my finger slipped off the hold button and I lost you and I didn't know where. . . ."

I bellowed, "Stop sniveling, you brainless twit. Let me talk to Bob!!"

She whined, "He just left."

Now, as I mentioned, during the morning I had taken seven pages of notes, single-spaced, both sides. In the afternoon I had produced nothing but doodles and filthy words. I figure I lost $150 because I was physically at a seminar yet mentally absent. That's no big deal. I'll get another $150. What I'll never get back is the half-day of my life I wasted because I failed to heed the rule: *Wherever you are,* *be there.*

At 5:30, when I got back to my office, there was a note from Bob Walker. "Sorry about the mix-up. Hope it didn't inconvenience you. I'll spring for lunch tomorrow." The problem had solved itself without me, as many do. In fact, problems come in two varieties: those which solve themselves and those which will wait for you. Let's face it, if there's a big alligator in your office and he doesn't go away, he'll wait for you to come in.

Most success books I've read focus a lot on money, as has this one. I suggest that that's not the whole game. Let me tell you about John. He started in real estate in 1958, in Los Altos, California, when I did. While I was spending my money on motorcycles, booze, little cars with no tops, slow horses, and fast women (the rest of the money I just wasted), he was buying real estate. He never sold any, just bought it and kept it. I had lunch with John a while ago. He had, under construction, for his own account, *twenty-six* industrial buildings. His income last year was half a million dollars—a *month*. Folks in our area say, "John's done well."

John just built a new office for himself. It has a bedroom and a shower and what-all. Good. He spends 16 to 20 hours per day in that office, six days a week. He's on his third marriage and in the process of getting out of that one. He lost a third of his stomach to an ulcer, aggravated by the fifth of scotch he drinks every day. His last vacation was two weeks in Phoenix, in a de-tox center.

How's John doing?

In traveling around the world, I've noticed a universal truth. They don't put luggage racks on hearses.

The best definition of success I've ever found was written by Robert Louis Stevenson a long time ago. That's good, as that's when he was alive.

That man is a success,

who has lived well,
    laughed often and loved much;

who has gained the respect
of intelligent men
and the love of children;

who has filled his niche
and accomplished his task;

who leaves the world better
than he found it,
whether by an improved poppy,
a perfect poem
or a rescued soul;

who never lacked appreciation
of earth's beauty
or failed to express it;

who looked for the best in others
and gave the best he had.

Take good care of you. You're all you've got.